Niccolò
Machiavelli

Clizia

Niccolò
Machiavelli

Clizia

Translation and Notes by
Daniel T. Gallagher
Northern Illinois University

Introduction by
Robert K. Faulkner
Boston College

WAVELAND
PRESS, INC.

Prospect Heights, Illinois

For information about this book, write or call:

Waveland Press, Inc.
P.O. Box 400
Prospect Heights, Illinois 60070
(847) 634-0081

Preface

Machiavelli writes in the prologue to *Clizia* that comedies were invented for the dual purpose of amusing and benefiting an audience. The amusement of comedy, he indicates, is achieved by portraying funny or pathetic characters saying and doing silly or offensive things, while its benefit, directed especially at the young in the audience, customarily consists of instruction regarding the great variety of human vice, something which, he insists, can be presented with the greatest decency (*onesta grandissima*). In Machiavelli's understanding, then, comedy represents a union of lighthearted and grave intentions, encouraging laughter at the same time as it conveys a sober teaching about weighty matters. Moreover, as the final song of *Clizia* suggests, the customary decency and sobriety of comedic instruction may not exhaust the educational potential of this dramatic form, since Machiavelli alludes here to the presence in his comedy—beneath the "thin veil" of a pious moral teaching—of a further profit accessible to the quiet and attentive listener. A Machiavellian comedy is indeed a complex work of art.

It would seem that the responsibility of the translator of such a comedy is to maximize the audience's access to the various dimensions of the play, enabling readers and listeners to derive pleasure from the jokes, for sure, but also making possible the careful and serious study of the work that is required to uncover fully its educational benefit. In my judgment, this responsibility is best fulfilled by means of a literal translation of the original text which, within the confines of readable English, grants an audience unimpeded access to what the author actually wrote, free of editorial interpretation, revision or correction. This new translation of *Clizia* tries to live up to this responsibility by presenting a faithful English reproduction of the Italian text, avoiding the temptation to simplify what was meant to be ambiguous, beautify what was meant to be offensive, or otherwise please the audience's ear at the expense of fidelity to the author's words. It must, however, be noted that this pursuit of a literal translation carries a certain cost in terms of textual clarity and intelligibility: Machiavelli's Renaissance vernacular contains terms and expressions that leave even Italian editors speculating as to their meaning, and the play abounds with proverbial sayings, parochialisms and time-bound references that are sure to bewilder contemporary English readers, obstructing rather than facilitating their access to the author's thought. In an effort to eliminate these obstacles without compromising the faithfulness of the translation, I have chosen to leave Machiavelli's play just as he wrote it and to supply notes that offer alternative translations for ambiguous words and explanations or contemporary stage translations for references that are likely to be unfamiliar to the reader. I am grateful to Mera Flaumenhaft of St. John's College, Annapolis, who read the translation with a careful eye and suggested a number of changes to improve both its accuracy and readability. Of course, I bear full responsibility for whatever errors might remain.

The translation is based on the Italian text of *Clizia* in Niccolò Machiavelli, *Opere Letterarie* (ed. Luigi Blasucci), Milan, 1964, which is in turn based on the text in *Tutte le opere storiche e letterarie di Niccolò Machiavelli* (ed. G. Mazzoni and M. Casella), Florence, 1929. While most of the annotation for this edition is new, I have, where useful and appropriate, translated explanatory notes offered both in the Blasucci edition and in Machiavelli, *Le Commedie* (*La Mandragola, Clizia*) (ed. Domenico Guerri), Torino, 1932.

I wish to thank the Social Sciences and Humanities Research Council of Canada for a postdoctoral fellowship awarded during the period in which this translation was completed, and the Government Department of Harvard University for a postdoctoral affiliation that granted me access to the Harvard Libraries.

Daniel T. Gallagher
DeKalb, Illinois

Introduction

Clizia and the Enlightenment of Private Life

A Machiavellian Play?

The *Clizia* is a comedy about love that borders on the scandalous. As a matter of fact, it crosses the border. But the play is not the ordinary romantic farce or, what is now more conventional, the ordinary artistic scandal. One would be foolish to expect the ordinary from a playwright so extraordinary. This Niccolò Machiavelli is the political thinker Machiavelli (1469–1527), a thinker known widely but known also as deep. While "Machiavellianism" has become a common term for a policy of unscrupulous but calculated force and fraud, Machiavelli is also said to be a political scientist or political philosopher. His famous *The Prince* is both the most influential handbook of policy ever written and the most influential treatise of political philosophy ever written. Machiavelli's dramas are similar, I think. They too mix common appeal and instruction with uncommon appeal and instruction. *Clizia* is raucous, but it is also maliciously witty about religion and morals. It teaches how to get the girl, but it also teaches how to manage loving and mating and a whole household. *Clizia* teaches a lot—if we can figure it out.[1]

It may seem funny to take seriously a comedy. And yet good comedy has to have a serious side. If you laugh at the low and the foolish, you must have some inkling of the high and the knowing. The more uncommon the playwright's grasp of such things, the more penetrating his humor and his drama. To that extent comedy inevitably instructs as it amuses, and uncommon playwrights mean it so. Machiavelli, our uncommon author here, certainly meant to instruct. A comic writer must devise "expressions which excite laughter," he wrote in a characteristically insidious tone, but the spectators, who attend to "enjoy themselves," will "taste afterwards the useful lesson that lay underneath."[2]

What useful lessons does Machiavelli advance beneath the biting humor of the *Clizia*? Are they related to the striking political lessons of, say, *The Prince*? And is there a distinctive Machiavellian humor designed to spread such lessons, to make them bite into the memory of a broad range of spectators?

During his lifetime Machiavelli's chief political works were not published (although manuscripts circulated). He was then generally known as statesman and diplomat and also from a variety of histories, essays, and, not least, works of imaginative fiction. The literary works included satiric and racy poems, satiric and racy stories, a translation (more or less) of a Roman play, and two original plays—*Clizia* and *The Mandragola*. A saucy little novella, *Belfagor*, became legendary in Italy. It told how the devil, come to earth, was conquered like all men by the trials of marriage. But it is the raucous comedies that have led some commentators to call Machiavelli the "greatest dramatist of his age," the "greatest of Italian dramatists," and a seminal influence upon later European playwrights such as Ben Jonson and William Congreve.[3]

On first sight, perhaps, the plot of *Clizia* demands little consideration. An old geezer, Nicomaco, has suddenly fallen for the beautiful Clizia, a girl of seventeen brought up from childhood in his household. But Nicomaco has to contend with his resourceful wife Sofronia and with his son Cleandro, who also wants to bed Clizia. The plot of the play moves through Nicomaco's plots and the others' counterplots. The old man would marry off Clizia to a pliable servant, Pirro, who will make the girl available to his master. But the wife Sofronia, who has stopped Cleandro by command, would stop Nicomaco by a countermarriage of Clizia to Eustachio, the stinky steward ("perfumed in dung") of the family farm. Nicomaco responds with a bizarre drawing of lots (with allusions to providential control); his Pirro wins out over Eustachio for the marriage rights. But Sofronia crowns this move by substituting a disguised male servant, Siro, for the "bride" Clizia. What Nicomaco finds in the marital bed is not what he had expected. There follows a lewdly humiliating encounter in the dark. The threat of bringing it to light is enough to bring Nicomaco to heel. At the end the unexpected arrival of a wealthy and respectable father of Clizia persuades Sofronia to allow Cleandro to marry Clizia. Through her wits and plots, and some help from chance, Sofronia manages to arrange a restored family and even a new and future prosperity.

It seems simple and even the triumph of justice. But there are strange loose ends in the plot. Why does Clizia never appear? Why does Clizia's father, Ramondo, appear out of nowhere? Why does Cleandro's friend, Palamede, completely disappear after his prominence in the first scene? And why the strange linkages of Nicomaco to God? One is also struck by the universality of selfish motives and calculating policies. How can there be a restoration of the family when each and every member is an instrument of private passion, be it sexual desire or an appetite for wealth, respectability, and security? And why the amorality or immorality in most or all of the chief characters and in their constant conspiring? The calculating tone seems intentional, not merely conventional. For it is matched by a theory of comedy expounded in the prologue.

Both of Machiavelli's original plays have prologues that are odd mixtures of the singularly self-regarding and the singularly theoretical. In *Clizia*'s prologue, the author speaks and mentions no predecessors, and he speaks as wise in the manner of a philosopher (as a knower of "events always the same" and hence of the nature of human things). This mixture is in contrast to the play on which *Clizia* is modeled, *Casina* by the Roman playwright Plautus.[4] In *Casina* the actors deliver the prologue and trace the play deferentially to a Greek original. But in *Clizia* the author tacitly sneers at traditional literary theories (as in Aristotle's *Poetics*) and recommends a cynical-scoffing comedy.[5] He calls for a comedy that is cynical about morals in particular, one which ridicules the supposition that being moral is realistic. Comedies were invented to "benefit" as well as to "delight," for thus the author can bring out the "avarice," "passion," and "tricks" in his characters. He can bring out, in general, "the untrustworthiness of all men." This kind of enlightenment as to allegedly real motives is reminiscent of Machiavelli's political theorizing. In a characteristic passage *The Prince* suggests that since all men are "wicked and do not observe faith with you," you need not keep faith with them (xviii; all quotations of *The Prince* are from the translation by Harvey C. Mansfield, Jr. [Chicago and London: University of Chicago Press, 1985], references are to chapters). Good faith (and justice in general) is an unrealistic hope and guide. For "it is so far from how one lives to how one should live"—according to the most famous formulation—"that he who lets go of what is done for what should be done learns his ruin rather than his preservation" (xv). But *The Prince* contains another side with other guidance. It contains an art of management with a foundation other than justice. If you concentrate not on governing with a view to what is good and fair, but on managing the passions and trickery that move men most powerfully, you can succeed and can preserve yourself. The play *Clizia* may scoff at scruples and religious faith. This cynical flavor is its distinctively Machiavellian "delight" and part of its benefit. But the play also shows how human beings in search of love and security may use one another to their mutual gain. This is the positive benefit. Machiavellian comedy shows how to succeed in private life.

Admittedly, some scholars will object to interpreting Machiavelli's comedies about private affairs with a view to the cynicism and arts of his politics. They have a point. How can a politics so grim give rise to humor? Machiavelli's political writings openly recommend cruelty in preference to mercy, and the art of being not merely bad, a murderer, but altogether bad, a murderer even of the pope and all the cardinals.[6] In view of teachings so chilling, some commentators on the comedies disavow any deeper meaning, especially a moral-political meaning. Art for art's sake, literature for literature's sake, and Machiavellian comedy for the sake of literary play in language.[7] But this proposal is impossible. To save the humor it dulls the humor, for it leads the reader away from Machiavelli's telling thrusts at, say, priests, gentlemen, Aristotle, and providence. Besides, such arty theorizing is contradicted by the *Clizia*'s theory of the "benefits" of comedy and Machiavelli's general subordination of humor to useful lessons.[8]

A Renaissance Play?

Many commentators agree that *Clizia* means to teach, but deny that its lessons are distinctively "Machiavellian." They describe the play as part of the Renaissance, and its instruction as merely what would be expected from the recovery of Greek and Roman drama and philosophy. Their chief evidence is the obvious fact that *Clizia* is a variation on Plautus's *Casina*, which is itself a variation on a Greek comedy.[9] In the Roman play *Casina*, as in *Clizia*, an old father competes with his son for the bed of a young ward, father and son try to marry the girl to competing servants, and the father is foiled by his wife. One might also note that *Clizia* abounds with allusions to Greek things. The Florentine incident recounted in *Clizia* is compared with a like event in ancient Athens. "Sofronia" is reminiscent of the Greek word for temperance or moderation (*Sōphrosunē*). "Doria," the name of the female servant who laughs so at her master's fall, is reminiscent of the Dorians, the Hellenic race that ruled in Sparta and the Greek cities of the Peloponnesus. "Palamede," the name of the wary friend of Cleandro, reminds of Palamedes, a legendary Greek wise man. "Nicomaco," "Cleandro," and "Eustachio" are Italian versions of Greek names.

Still, such surface similarities with Roman and Greek things are inconclusive, for in other writings Machiavelli can be seen to manipulate classical allusions for innovative ends. *The Mandragola* radically revises the legend of Lucretia's rape by the Roman tyrant Tarquin, and *Discourses on Livy* continually revises the Roman historian Titus Livy's account of Rome. To such considerations one might reply that *Clizia* is different; it is neoclassical in manifest contrast to the earlier works.[10] In ridiculing old Nicomaco's lusts, *Clizia* is a "critique of aggressive *virtù*." It is thus precisely a critique of the "Machiavellianism" that governed *The Prince*, *Discourses*, and *The Mandragola*. According to this contention, *Clizia* stands out in recurring to the ancients' praise of moral virtue and especially of moderation. A name intimates the change of heart. "Nicomaco" is said to combine parts of the author's two names, and his humiliation to exhibit Niccolò Machiavelli's self-punishment for his earlier excesses.

Unfortunately for such a resourceful argument, two big difficulties stand in the way of any attempt to interpret *Clizia* as a restoration of ancient morals. First, there are major differences from Plautus's *Casina*, and they go in a Machiavellian direction. While *Casina* basically ridicules an old man's vice, *Clizia*, whatever its critique of old Nicomaco, has an additional theme. It is also a how-to-do-it play on a topic of interest to young men: how to succeed in bedding young women. In Plautus's play the son never appears. In *Clizia* Cleandro's sexual hunt helps to set the play in motion (I.1) (as Callimaco's does in *The Mandragola*). Both of Machiavelli's plays blend young passions with old heads. They thus teach how to do it reliably and with a view to more important considerations (that is, for the long haul, and without sacrificing security). Security is somehow primary, while love is but a force to be satisfied at others' expense or to be otherwise managed. In Plautus's play the distinctive metaphor for love is food; in Machiavelli's, it is war.[11] In Plautus's play the mother, while thwarting her husband, also sympathizes with her son's love and promotes it. In *Clizia* mother thwarts son as well as husband for her own purpose, that is, until a marriage useful to the family may be obtained. It is a mother's *ambizione* as well as a father's lust that stands in Cleandro's way (V.5; cf. II.3,4).

Second, and the important point, the lessons of the play are not about the virtue of moderation, but about realism with respect to motives and management. Nicomaco's passion is ridiculed as feeble and ineffectual, not as incestuous and evil. *Casina* had concluded with the shaming of vice, but without much visible effect; merciless ridicule from servants and wife hardly made the old man repentant. The Roman play contains no hint of the domestic reconstitution that concludes *Clizia*. Machiavelli's play ends with a political success in the household, a success that arises from a political-theological revolution. The wife ends up completely in charge, and the cause is her schemes, not her morals and piety. Nicomaco acknowledges his subordination because he has to; he has been intimidated. But the new ruler, Sofronia, is nevertheless understanding about Nicomaco's excesses and shrewd about her remedy. She understands his excesses less as vices to be morally condemned and more as forces to be expected. She perceives that only force shrewdly applied can correct them. Besides, Nicomaco too had feared to turn the household "bottoms-up" (II.2). Thus reconciled to their necessities by her management and his own fear, the two retire to a household restored, or, rather, secured on a new basis. Indeed, the household will be advanced. This too is due to Sofronia's planning. All along Sofronia has treated Clizia as a potential asset; she exclaims against "throwing away" the girl on whom "they have expended so much effort" (II.3). As soon as Clizia is known to have a father rich and noble, as well as accepting of Cleandro, no other questions are asked. *Casina* has no parallels to this concluding affirmation, in a comedy of love, of the primacy of riches and respectability. The *Clizia* ends by showing how human necessities can be effectively managed to a certain mutual satisfaction. It eschews moral indignation because it has eschewed morality—and any moral seriousness of love.

In short, the *Clizia* is less a recovery of the old Greek and Roman wisdom than a corrosive satire on it. While from its first song the play does veil itself in "ancient" or "very ancient" themes, these are an ironic disguise for ingenious attacks on the morals of a Renaissance audience. The play takes aim especially at Greek philosophy in its Christian version. Consider Nicomaco. He is a respectable Christian gentleman who looks up to "ancient and modern examples" for the instruction of his son. But his mixture of ancient virtue and modern religion is shown to be no match for his passions. If one would play around with names, "Nicomaco" reminds rather directly of the *Nicomachean Ethics* of Aristotle, which takes the gentleman as moral model. The *Ethics* is *the* philosophic defense of good character, that is, of moral virtue. It was supposedly addressed to Aristotle's son, Nicomachus. Might Machiavelli hint maliciously that Aristotle's moralism denies to young sons the pleasures that fathers secretly desire and would appropriate for themselves?

Lessons in Scoffing

Even the fluffy surface of *Clizia* innovates within Renaissance convention. The fluffiest of the fluff are the songs (*Casina* had none), and they bespeak a world of force and fraud only loosely covered by conventional romance and piety. The first song features pagan nymphs and shepherds mooning nostalgically over their antique loves. The last song sardonically eulogizes the play as a "wise and noble teacher" that shows what is needed for "ascending to heaven"—and then for teaching "under a veil a great deal more." Between such veils, the first ironically pagan and the last sardonically Christian, are four songs that treat of love, youthful ardor, woman's anger at offense, and trickery. The songs alone teach a great deal more. They treat love, ardor, and the rest simply as forces, and such forces as the real "lords." These are passions that overpower decency and that overpower gods as well as men. Love may bring heaven's "highest worth," and the love in question is the "great power" that men and gods dread. It is a power in the bodies of the "ardent young," not of the old. A yet superior force is vengeance, especially female vengeance. A woman offended, whether "wrongly or with reason," is full of pride, anger, trickery, and cruelty; her force is more than "all mortal force." There seems to be a still bigger force: the fraud of trickery. The successful trick obtains the highest tribute paid in these songs. It is the "remedy high and rare" that "shows the straight path to wandering souls." Great trickery, the conspiracy that works, seems to be Machiavelli's replacement for the undying claims of the good and the divine. It alone can bring a lasting state of satisfaction.

This turn to an orientation by "real" forces presupposes the profound critique of morals found in Machiavelli's most important works, notably in chapter xv of *The Prince*. The special task of the comedies is to package that critical thinking for a popular audience. In the prologue to *Clizia*, Machiavelli appears not only as philosopher but also as both brutally authoritative director of the actors and indirect director of the audience. He orders the actors out front and, as if speaking for "the people," back off-stage. This comedy is insistent about what is put before the audience, and yet it puts itself in the people's shoes. Machiavelli makes himself the instrument—the people's voice—for their desires. He thus directs to enlightened satisfaction, rather than moral and religious duty. But such a reductive message depends on a prior critique of the moral spirit, such as the spirit governing the *Casina*. That is why "scoffing" at morals is central to Machiavellian laughter. The prologue ends by defending the immorality (*disonesta*) of the play for those who might find it immoral, especially women. It is the defense of immorality that calls forth the new theory of comedy. Comedy pleases by ridiculing pretensions, especially the professing of decency, the pretension of acting according to what one ought to do. The *Clizia* is quiet about incest and chastity—while outraging modesty with its sensational conclusion.

In *Clizia* one sees the reductionist view of love now powerful among the literati of modern lands: sexual desire accompanied by fantasy. The real thing is the sexual urge, which is itself some mixture of desire for pleasure and desire for domination. What men think they ought to love, and thus the special beauty and character of the person they love, is mere fantasy. Love, insofar as distinct from sexual passion, is a mere imagining. It is to be dismissed by serious people. The two most serious people in *Clizia* are Palamede and Sofronia, and they both dismiss it. Replying to Cleandro in heat, Palamede would avoid lovers and musicians (as well as old people). When Cleandro wails to Sofronia that he must be satisfied, Sofronia tells him that he can wait to be satisfied. She plans to marry him off to someone else or wait until his fantasy dissipates (V.4; cf. V.3; III.3).

In Cleandro and Nicomaco alike there is nothing of the lover chastened in his desire by awe before the qualities of his beloved. When in Shakespeare's *Tempest* the prince Ferdinand sees young and beautiful Miranda, he looks up to her as a "goddess." "O you wonder," he breathes (I.2). When Miranda's father warns about "th' fire ith' blood," Ferdinand says, to some

skepticism from the father, that he would not "melt Mine honor
into lust" (IV.i). Love as honorable love is absent from *Clizia*.
"Honor," in the sense of reverence for something high or
worthy, is absent as a motive. Neither Cleandro nor Nicomaco
looks up to Clizia's goodness (to which Sofronia alone refers
[II.3]). While Cleandro and Pirro certainly drool over Clizia's
"delicate" charms (IV.1; II.5), this is anticipation of a delectable
dish. The men show no awe before her beauty and certainly no
concern for charm and seriousness of soul. The steward
Eustachio even calculates that a beautiful wife can always be
a source of income (III.5). The women are not much different.
Sostrata jokes at Clizia's presumed scruples about lovemaking
(IV.10). Sofronia refers to this "good and beautiful girl," but she
treats these attributes as qualities useful for the market, that
is, as making the girl a commodity that they should make the
most out of. Some such considerations probably explain why
Clizia is referred to as but an imagining (*fantasia*) and never
really appears on stage (I.1; II.4; V.3). Beauty and goodness are
but images of wish-fulfillment, for Cleandro as well as Nicomaco.

The Machiavellian critique of love extends to friendship and
perhaps to love of wisdom as well. A key example is Palamede.
The Greek Palamedes was a legendary wise man who is
supposed to have invented great benefactions, such as light-
houses and the alphabet, but to have come to a bad end
because of his supposed friends. He was induced by the wily
Odysseus to join the expedition to recover Helen of Troy,
according to one version of the Trojan legend. He was betrayed
by the leaders, including Odysseus and perhaps King Agamem-
non himself.[12] Some clues in *Clizia* hint at Machiavelli's im-
proved version of the wise benefactor. This Palamede is secretive,
occupied with his own "business," and wary of helping others
(especially lovers and musicians). He will help only if "necessary." He does not help except to advise temporizing in the face
of superior forces. The wary secretiveness of Palamede and
Cleandro is a little Machiavellian commentary on friendship.
Strictly speaking, friendship does not exist, since no one acts
knowingly for another or loves good things (such as knowledge)
that inherently can be shared. Cleandro seeks help in his
necessity; he tells of his necessity in order to vent his passion,

to get it off his chest (I.1; IV.1). Machiavellian friendship is trust or aid by those who need to gain something from one another. Palamede does not need to serve Cleandro, although he offers. Cleandro's affairs are not put in order except by Sofronia, whose necessities encompass his.

Lessons in Management

Since everyone strives for personal gain, according to Machiavelli, without inherent limits on desire except for the limits of possibility, each must fight for personal satisfaction. In love as in war, the key art is of war. In *Clizia* Cleandro compares lover to soldier (I.2). Sofronia would defend Clizia from the "camps" of husband, son, and servants alike (I.3). There are sexually charged analogies with conquest and the weapons of war (I.1; II.1, 3; IV.5, 11, 12; etc.). Actually, love is war according to Machiavelli, except, I suppose, as its pleasures make soft and enduring submission preferable to forced submission, that is, to rape. Cleandro and Nicomaco seek the conquest of Clizia. Cleandro wants her in any way possible (I.1). Cleandro and Nicomaco are desperate, one to the point of willing death and the other to breaking up his whole household and burning down his house. But there is no moral misery, that is, disgust at one's baseness or despair at losing something admirable. There is only the misery that fears failure and that spurs the search for the strategy and tactics of victory.

Victory in love as in war requires allies and so incentives—hence the need for management. What the young Cleandro more or less lacks on his own is ingenious stratagems or tricks, the "remedies" that Nicomaco and Sofronia manage to devise. One needs fraud as well as force, for if life is a battle, it is not least a battle of wits. *Clizia* shows how shrewd elders like Sofronia may earn the trust of the young by showing youthful passions the road to long-term satisfaction. Leaders can serve themselves in managing followers.

In *Clizia* Sofronia alone exhibits the *virtù* of a leader. Of all the characters, she alone uses the word and she defines it, while referring to a prospective son-in-law, in Machiavellian fashion. *Virtù* is "knowing how to do something" that will provide for "business," the household, "or the affairs of others and himself" (II.3). *Virtù* is the ability to provide. It amounts to self-reliance broadly construed. Sofronia also has *industria* (I.1), a concentration on one's advancement, which is a more basic attitude or passion that underlies *virtù*.[13] These crucial Machiavellian qualities do not revolve about *onesta*, about decency or moderation. They focus on ability to master oneself and one's environment, an ability to provide for oneself and others. While Sofronia's *virtù* may be within domestic limits, she exhibits a characteristically Machiavellian self-reliance.

At first Sofronia seems a more traditional woman: dependent upon others, moral, and pious. She looks for remedies from Cleandro and from God; she "would do good all the time" and goes off to mass (II.3); she retains a certain subordination to husband as well as household. But from the start her churchgoing is linked with a statement that she "does not want to submit" her affairs "to anyone" (II.3). When Sofronia returns from mass she is full of schemes, not piety, and threatens to expose and humiliate her husband (II.3). By play's end Sofronia is fierce in devising her own remedies for the security of herself and her household. This mixture of spiritedness with cynicism and inventiveness is Machiavellian *virtù*.

Sofronia exhibits in her own way the mastery of fortune that is a prominent theme in *Clizia*. It is Nicomaco who believes in good fortune and puts his hopes in a lottery (III.6). He seems to mix Aristotelian reliance on nature's goodness with religious reliance on help from providence. According to Cleandro, however, fortune is an obstacle and is to be conquered (IV.1; V.5). He repeats a theme of the notorious *The Prince*: fortune, like a woman, is a "friend of the young" (IV.1). *The Prince* explains that the young are less timid and thus command fortune "with more audacity," but it also indicates that audacity has its limits (xxv). *Clizia* (and *The Mandragola*) show the limitations of forceful young studs carried away by passion and without the ingenuity needed when up against superior forces.

Sofronia's art of managing fortune is a domesticated art of war; she contrives forces to intimidate her husband. She contrives ingeniously, and her forces break his power and then reconstitute it for her purposes. Having utterly humiliated Nicomaco before witnesses from the household, she can keep him "humble" through his fear of exposure. We see a version of the fundamental intimidation discussed in Machiavelli's political works.[14] Any society needs a periodic recurrence to its "foundations." This is Machiavellian idiom for return to an original fear, indeed, to a founding terror. The foundation of society is directed terror, which so sinks into selfish men as to make them obey something other than themselves. "Men will always turn out bad for you unless they have been made good by a necessity."[15] *The Prince's* most famous example of well-used terror is Cesare Borgia, who laid "very good foundations" for his rule (vii). Borgia engaged in acts of intimidation that culminated in spectacularly terrifying, but pointed, executions. He first set up a "cruel and ready" prosecutor to pacify the land, that is, to destroy the robbers and murderers who had flourished under impotent "lords." This subordinate having done his work, and having provoked his own enmities and resentments, was found in a piazza "in two pieces" with a piece of wood and a bloody knife. "The ferocity of this spectacle left the people at once satisfied and stupefied." Sofronia's management involves no murder, which would have been hardly conducive to laughter. But it does effect a spectacular sexual humiliation that serves to destroy the old man's domestic tyranny and to unify a reformed household.

Enlightened Household, Enlightened Women

The household as alliance: this marks the *Clizia's* radical reform of the pretensions of fathers and masters and the dutifulness of mothers and servants. A fatherly claim to reverence as *paterfamilias* appears particularly pretentious in light of the real motives and trickiness to be seen in a Nicomaco.[16] Wife and son lose their illusions and thus their awe. They learn to penetrate to real motives of men, fathers or no. According to Cleandro, his father is "the foundation and cause of my harm" (III.1). Nicomaco, checked by public enlightenment as to his real motives, may then be kept in the useful harness of domestic provider.

Nicomaco's status as lordly master declines with that of sacred father. *Clizia*, one might say, is a continual deconstruction by ridicule of the traditional master-servant relation. One sign of the new attitudes is the servant Doria's strangely exaggerated laughter at her master's humiliation; another sign is her extended triumphing at this "beautiful trick" (IV.8; V.1). But the paradigmatic example is the triumph of Siro the servant, who sets upon Nicomaco in the ultimate male gesture of contempt. The story of Nicomaco's humiliations by Siro, sexual and otherwise, is the most sensational action of the play. All enjoy this overturn of the master, but the play dwells on the servants' enjoyment. Machiavelli may not proceed down the legalistic and economic road taken by John Locke, who meant to turn the hierarchical relation between master and servant into a contractual relation between employer and employee. Nevertheless, insofar as service and servants are to remain in the Machiavellian order, the traditional expectation of reverence and dutifulness will be subverted by hidden disdain and by the supposition of natural equality in ends and urges. Machiavelli would destroy the case for servile deference to gentlemen. He would replace the old hierarchical family with a managed association that appeals to mutual utility.

Both of Machiavelli's plays foster a liberation of women that seems eerily contemporary. In *The Mandragola* the beautiful wife, Lucrezia, is liberated from husband and modesty to take power and a lover in her household. In *Clizia* the old wife, Sofronia, rises from equivocal subordination before lord and master to rule the whole household on which she depends. The last two acts of *Clizia* are almost "entirely in the control of women,"[17] including the servant Doria and the offstage Clizia. But this Machiavellian liberation has a rationalism about it, a cool planning for security through association, that is alien to much contemporary feminism. It is Sofronia's cool inventiveness as to politic schemes that establishes her control. She is not overcome by fear, she scoffs at Nicomaco's transparent efforts to win her with love, and she keeps her wits when Cleandro loses his. While she schemes to ridicule her husband for her purposes, she avoids offending him when he is cowed, also for her purposes. Sofronia needs her husband for her family and its respectability and wealth. Machiavellian liberation is an enlightened liberation, one that encourages a calculated concern for the long term. Old Sofronia is the most Machiavellian character in the play, most like the author of the play (as is Ligurio in *The Mandragola*). She is the brains of the job. But it is true that the cool lewdness of the play also contributes to Machiavelli's liberation of women, especially from the constraints of decency.

Clizia and The Mandragola

What is the relation of *Clizia* to the more famous *The Mandragola*?[18] Commentators have discussed whether it is inferior as a literary work, and yet the question of substantive relationship is rarely raised. How does the plot and teaching of *Clizia* complement, contradict, or duplicate that of *The Mandragola*? It is a question provoked by *Clizia* itself. Two similar characters of the same name (Sostrata and Siro) had appeared before in *The Mandragola*. Two songs (as to the power of love and of trickery) had appeared as well. More significant, Nicomaco expressly reminds Sofronia of Frate Timoteo's miracle-working in *The Mandragola* (to produce Lucrezia's pregnancy), slyly suggesting that they allow the (corruptible) friar to pick the servant who gets to marry Clizia (II.3).

This incident is a clue to the relation of the plays. In *The Mandragola* the pious Lucrezia is bedded adulterously only after the friar salved her conscience with theological casuistry. But in *Clizia* the female lead scoffs, and lewdly: "As if one needed a miracle to explain a priest getting a woman pregnant" (II.3). The general relation is this: in confronting the twin traditions from ancient Greece and Christian Rome, the *Clizia* concentrates its fire chiefly (but not solely) on Greek moral wisdom, *The Mandragola* more on Latin theological learning.

The British philosopher Edmund Burke once traced the European tradition of chivalry to a blend of the Greek tradition of the gentleman with the Christian tradition of piety. Both of

Machiavelli's plays take aim at this mix, and both fight on the battleground of love and the sexes. The common aim is shown by the common political context, the Italian situation familiar from Machiavelli's political diagnoses. Clizia had been found or won by a French captain during the invasion of Italy (1494) under the French king, Charles VIII. Callimaco (in *The Mandragola*) returns from Paris, where he had fled because of the same French invasion. Thus, both plays take their broad bearings from Italian political weakness, which Machiavelli symbolizes by this and other French incursions (*The Prince*, iii, vii, viii, xii). This is a characteristically modern weakness, Machiavelli seemed to think. It was caused by the pretensions to power of pacific Christian gentlemen and of an unarmed Roman Church that needs armed allies, including foreign kings. In addressing such paradoxes of morality at the level of romantic comedy, moreover, both plays play with the naturalness and force of sexual passion, as represented by the character named Sostrata. In *Clizia* and *The Mandragola* alike she laughs at scruple, counsels indulgence in pleasure, prepares the bride or wife for lovemaking, and is in on the conspiracy (*Clizia*, IV.2,10,12; *The Mandragola*, II.6; III.1,9,10,11; V.5,6).

In the common attack on religion and moral restraints, however, there is a certain concentration of labor, even if no strict division. Greek things and opinions are more prominent in *Clizia*: Athens, Greek names, a philosophic theory of comedy, and a wise friend. This play satirizes chiefly aristocratic morality, the gentleman and his household, deference to superiors, and the naturalness of governance by fathers and males in general. While *The Mandragola* does not spare morality as such, it is notable for addressing Christian morals; it is distinctive in attending to Latin names, Latin passages, and the Roman philosopher and statesman Boethius. Its special focus is on spirituality, Christian theology, chastity, the church, and the superiority of Christian husbands and priests. The title character in *Clizia* is never seen; the play spoofs as nonexistent the perfection that men (and not least Aristotelians) imagine to be the goal of natural desire. The title of *The Mandragola* (the mandrake-root) refers to a supposed medical cure that is shown to be a funny fraud; that play spoofs as nonexistent a miracle which was supposed to change nature and produce "a soul for our Lord" (III.11). Similarly, Clizia is left by a military gentleman and proves to be the daughter of a worldly gentleman. But Lucrezia in *The Mandragola* is distinguished by her devotion to God the Father and is married to a credulous Christian gentleman. In *Clizia* Sofronia uses Nicomaco's strange confidence in friends and in established hierarchies to overcome the chance result of his strange confidence in the drawing of lots. In *The Mandragola* Ligurio uses Nicia's faith in miraculous cures to overcome Lucrezia's faith in providence.

The different themes show themselves above all, or below all, in the different beddings. Both plays describe openly what decency would shroud, acts that challenge and undermine sexual awe and especially feminine modesty. Both episodes lead to a revolution in the household. *The Mandragola*'s recounting of Callimaco's night with Lucrezia describes what amounts to a blasphemous satire on conversion to Christ: an anti-religious conversion that follows an earlier black mass with Dr. Callimaco as high priest. Pious wife is transformed into enlightened woman. Lucrezia departs from faith in God, holy fathers, and husband. She turns to worldly pleasure, acceptance of her strong young lover as "lord and master," and domination beneath the facade of a traditional household. *Clizia*'s sexual spectacle, on the other hand, challenges particularly the presumptive naturalness of procreational sex and of the superiority of gentleman to servant. The final bedding of Nicomaco, if one can call it that, involves display of male intercourse, if one can call it that, and the power of a strong young servant over an old and foolish master. It symbolizes subversion of the aristocratic and paternal moral order—and of the Aristotelianism that upheld such an order as in accord, more or less, with the best in human nature.

There is some reason to think that *Clizia* is a completion of Machiavelli's comic project for managed liberation, not just a complement to other parts. The servant who triumphs is Siro. In *The Mandragola* a servant Siro appears as a perfect servant, so perfect as to seem unnatural. In that play we do not see Siro changed, despite the subversion of the Christian household, and despite the fact that Siro is often astute and is finally the object of Ligurio's solicitude: "Is there no man who remembers

Siro?" (V.6). In *Clizia* Machiavelli remembers the servant Siro. Siro triumphs, and his laughter ridiculing Nicomaco is expressly noted. It may be that *Clizia* subverts what Machiavelli thought to be the remaining and secular pillar of the traditional household, an allegedly natural superiority in fathers and masters.

Comedy of Enlightenment

In general, Machiavellian comedies promote for private life the reconstruction that *The Prince* and *Discourses* promote for public life. They subvert and they construct. They subvert the apparently natural or divine hierarchies of the household. They then construct artificial associations for private satisfactions. This private reform by comedy complements Machiavelli's public reform. In addition, it is an insinuating way of introducing through private attitudes the attitudes that bring public reform. Without reform we stint ourselves, in the words of the first song—are "repressed," as we say today. The plays enlighten us to think instead that we are put upon in the name of the old fogies and dominating creeds of the world.

The young, strong, clever, and female have been especially put upon, according to the plays, and Machiavellian comedy aims especially to liberate and instruct them. Women are primary beneficiaries, with young playboys probably in second place. Both Sofronia and Lucrezia are pretty much in control of their households by play's end. "Whoever offends a woman" must face a force that surpasses "all mortal force," according to the song after act III of *Clizia*, and Machiavelli takes his own warning to heart. This first of modern political philosophers caters to women in the prologue to *Clizia*, and both comedies are chiefly for their liberation and instruction.

The socially and politically prominent men, on the other hand, are by and large forgettable. They are boys preoccupied with girls or old men preoccupied with domestic security (or with girls). The male servants are no better; they are alternately cheeky and servile. It is true that Ligurio is the brains of *The Mandragola* and that other clever men are memorable, such as Father Timoteo in *The Mandragola* and to a lesser extent Palamede in *Clizia*. But all of these have instrumental roles. Some are conspirators, indeed, but chiefly for someone else's benefit. They get only partial satisfaction in managing another person's domestic satisfactions, although Ligurio gets a leg up in his rising. It may be that first-rate men wish the honor or glory of public life, a life which in its Machiavellian form is inevitably grave and ruthless. The pleasures and security of love and of the household are primarily for second-rate men and for almost all women (Lucrezia, "fit to govern a kingdom" [I.3] is an exception). Machiavellian comedy is principally for women and second-rate men.

In the prologue to *The Mandragola*, the author says that he engages in such "light" literary pursuits only because he is "cut off from showing with other enterprises other *virtù*." Machiavelli too gets only a secondary satisfaction from the domestic scene and from satisfying audiences with such stuff. A student must look to *The Prince* and *Discourses* to understand the scope of Machiavelli's singular outlook, not least as to first-rate men.

Still, the comedies are themselves a profound political innovation and make their own contribution to Machiavelli's grave enterprise of enlightenment. Comedy had not enjoyed a very good press among the political philosophers who preceded Machiavelli. They saw a short road between laughing at respectable people and officials, and losing reverence for morals and law. This road between satire and lawlessness or licentiousness is especially short for the young. Their character—their stance toward life and the passions—is comparatively unformed. Some ancient philosophers had worried about a slippery slope. Aristotle's *Politics* advises that in well-governed countries lampoons and comedies be kept from the young until their upbringing is completed ($1336^{b}20$–35). His *Poetics* exhibits similar apprehensions. The *Poetics* touches on the origins of comedy in Dionysian revels, phallic songs, primitive parodies, and crude invectives. It connects the rise of comedy with the rise of democracy and common tastes, and with wandering comedians dishonored in their towns ($1448^{a}32{,}36$–39, $1449^{a}12$–13). Still, these grave doubts are not Aristotle's only reflections on comic topics. The

Poetics defends a moral and philosophic comedy, and the *Nicomachean Ethics* supplements this while praising wittiness as a virtue. Suitable comedy ridicules the low and warns about the power of the base (as Shakespeare's *Tempest* exposes Caliban and Antonio). It also illuminates the foibles of men from the heights of the wise; "Lord, what fools these mortals be." There is high comedy as well as low comedy. High comedy illuminates foolishness as well as baseness, preparing the mind for discriminating judgments about the advantages and disadvantages of different ways of life. It encourages a serious thoughtfulness that is philosophic. Great comedies such as the *Tempest* contribute to the pleasure of knowing as well as the pleasure of laughing.[19]

Machiavelli's is different comedy, although it too means to instruct. It instructs in policy and being politic. It does not ridicule the low, except as short-sighted, but it especially ridicules those who pretend to be high, that is, to be virtuous, spiritual, or superior in elevated wisdom. It is less high comedy than low comedy, because it disdains the distinction between noble and base. But ultimately it is neither, for it exposes above all the foolishness of high and low that keeps each from the effectual ways of real satisfaction, which it also shows. It does elevate the wise, but in the cool form of the shrewd.

Hence, Machiavellian comedy is peculiarly cynical and peculiarly conspiratorial and rational. Its humor is in exposing the pretension in others' airs of superiority and in enjoying one's own superiority in tricks and plots. This twofold wit, malicious and proud, is characteristically Machiavellian. *The Prince* and *Discourses* may be grim by the standards of ordinary morals and politics. But they are enlivened with the pleasure of unveiling and surpassing well-meaning men and even the evil princes who pride themselves on vice. Machiavelli's comedy is then farther from low comedy than is, say, Shakespeare's. There is an easy warmth about Shakespeare's; consider Stephano and Trinculo in the *Tempest*, or Bottom in *Midsummer Night's Dream*. Machiavelli's is cold if raucous in its use of the ridiculous, for it is calculatingly in the service of an artificial and politic reform.[20] The *Clizia* is a comic classic of enlightened rhetoric, a classic insinuation of the critique and the planning that underlie modern free society as well as modern effective government.

Robert K. Faulkner
Auburndale, Massachusetts

Notes

[1] I am grateful for Mera J. Flaumenhaft's many corrections and for helpful suggestions from Kent Cochrane, Daniel Gallagher, and Sharon Johnson.

[2] *Dialogue on Language,* in J. R. Hale, ed. and transl., *The Literary Works* (Westport, CT: Greenwood Press, 1979), 188.

[3] J. R. Hale, in *The Literary Works,* xxvi; Daniel C. Boughner, *The Devil's Disciple, Ben Jonson's Debt to Machiavelli* (New York: Philosophical Library, 1968).

[4] Titus Maccius Plautus (c. 254–184 BC). Twenty-one of Plautus's comedies survive.

[5] According to one commentator, Machiavelli "invented the critical prologue in which the author does something never met in classical literature: he analyzes and discusses his own art" (Boughner, *The Devil's Disciple,* 12).

[6] *The Prince,* xii, xvii; *Discourses on the First Decade of Titus Livy,* I.27.

[7] Hale, *The Literary Works,* xii.

[8] *Dialogue on Language,* in Hale, *The Literary Works,* 188.

[9] *Clerumenae* (The lot drawers), a lost work by Diphilus.

[10] See Ronald L. Martinez, "Benefit of Absence: Machiavellian Valediction in *Clizia,*" in Albert Russell Ascoli and Victoria Kahn, eds., *Machiavelli and the Discourse of Literature* (Ithaca and London: Cornell University Press, 1993).

[11] Marvin T. Herrick, *Italian Comedy in the Renaissance* (Urbana: University of Illinois Press, 1960), 45.

[12] See Sir William Smith's account in *A Classical Dictionary of Greek and Roman Biography, Mythology, and Geography,* rev. G. E. Marindin (London: John Murray, 1919).

[13] See Mansfield's commentary in *The Prince,* ii, n.4.

[14] *Discourses on Livy,* I.4,5; see especially Martin Fleischer, "Trust and Deceit in Machiavelli's Comedies," *Journal of the History of Ideas,* vol. 27, no. 3, pp. 365–80; also Martinez, "Machiavellian Valediction in *Clizia,*" 120; and Timothy Lukes, "Fortune Comes of Age (in Machiavelli's *Literary Works*)," *Sixteenth Century Journal,* vol. 11, no. 4 [1980], esp. pp. 44–45.

[15] *The Prince,* xxiii.

[16] The ridicule may go theologically deep. Nicomaco calls himself "lord of his household" (III.1); "God" and such phrases as "in the name of God" and "stand with Christ" are attached to him; he is "dead" and "brought back to life" (III.6,7). Does the supposition that fathers are benevolent depend, according to Machiavelli, upon the supposition of governance by a good Father above?

[17] Martinez, "Machiavellian Valediction in *Clizia*," 131.

[18] All quotations of *The Mandragola* are from the translation by Mera Flaumenhaft (Prospect Heights, IL: Waveland Press, 1981). Consider also Flaumenhaft's "The Comic Remedy: Machiavelli's *Mandragola*," *Interpretation: A Journal of Political Philosophy*, vol. 7, no. 2 [1978].

[19] *Nicomachean Ethics*, 1127^b33–1128^b9. See Susan D. Collins, *The Ends of Action: The Moral Virtues in Aristotle's Nicomachean Ethics* (Ph.D. dissertation, Graduate School of Arts and Sciences, Boston College, 1994), 159–72.

[20] Lukes suggests that "the triviality and humor of the dramatic medium may have best suited Machiavelli's intentions—to relate truly revolutionary and immoral ideas without being labeled a gross revolutionary and atheist himself" ("Fortune Comes of Age," 37, n. 4). This is compatible with accurate perceptions by the clever of "how dangerous" such a play was "for a young man." Consider the first encounter with *The Mandragola* of the playwright Carlo Goldoni, who "devoured" it and immediately reread it "at least ten times" (*Memoirs of Carlo Goldoni*, trans. John Black [Boston: James Osgood and Company, 1877], 72).

Clizia

CHARACTERS

PALAMEDE   SOFRONIA
CLEANDRO   DAMONE
EUSTACHIO   DORIA
NICOMACO   SOSTRATA
PIRRO   RAMONDO

Song

Spoken before the comedy, by a nymph and shepherds together

How joyous is this day,
on which ancient memories are
by us displayed and celebrated,
we can see, because around us
all friendly people
are in this place assembled.
We, who spent our years
in forest and field,
have come here too,
I a nymph, and we who are shepherds,
singing together about our loves.

Clear are the days, and tranquil,
happy and beautiful the countryside,

1

where the sound of our song may be heard.
So, cheerful and joyous,
these enterprises of yours
we will accompany with our singing,
with such sweet harmony
as you have never heard before;
and then we will depart,
I a nymph, and we who are shepherds,
and return to our ancient loves.

PROLOGUE

If in the world the same men should return, just as the same events[1] return, never would a hundred years pass by without our finding ourselves together here once again to do the same thing as now.[2] This is said because once in Athens, a noble and very ancient city in Greece, there was a gentleman who had no children other than a boy, into whose house there chanced to arrive a little girl who, up to the age of seventeen, was raised by him in a very decent fashion.[3] Then it happened that all at once both he and his son fell in love with her; and in the competition of this love there arose many events and strange accidents,[4] upon whose passing the son took her as a wife and lived with her very happily for a long time.[5]

What would you say if this same case, just a few years ago, also took place in Florence? And since our author wanted to present one of the two to you, he chose the Florentine one, since he judged that you would get greater pleasure from this one than the other. For Athens is in ruins, her streets, her public squares, her sites are not recognizable to you. Moreover, her citizens spoke Greek, and you wouldn't understand that language. So take this case that occurred in Florence, but don't expect to recognize either the household or the people, because

---

[1] events: *casi* (sing. *caso*), elsewhere translated as "matters" or "affairs" when in the plural; "story," "case" or "chance" when in the singular.

[2] For Machiavelli's thoughts on the constancy of human affairs and the "things of the world," see *Discourses on Livy*, I.11 (end); I.39; III.43.

[3] very decent fashion: *onestissimamente. Onesta* refers to a general moral rectitude. It will be translated throughout as "decency."

[4] strange accidents: *strani accidenti*: curious and unforeseen events.

[5] Machiavelli alludes in this paragraph to Plautus's *Casina*, the Roman comedy on which the plot of *Clizia* is loosely based.

the author, in order to flee accusation,[6] has changed the real names to fictitious names.

Before the comedy begins he would like very much to have you see the characters, so that you might recognize them better as it is being performed.

[*To cast*] Come out here everyone, so that the people can see you.

Here they are. Do you see how agreeably they come along? [*To cast*] Place yourselves over there in a row, close together. You see. This first is Nicomaco, an old man all full of love. The one beside him is Cleandro, his son and rival. The other is named Palamede, a friend of Cleandro. Those two that follow, one is Pirro, a servant, the other Eustachio, a steward, each of whom would like to be the husband of his master's beloved. That woman who comes next is Sofronia, Nicomaco's wife; the one next to her is Doria, her maid. Of those final two that remain, one is Damone, the other is Sostrata, his wife. There is another character who, since he has yet to come from Naples, will not be shown to you. I believe this suffices; you have seen them enough.

[*To cast*] The people give you leave;[7] go back inside.

This tale is called *Clizia*, because this is the name of the young girl who is being fought over. Don't expect to see her, because Sofronia, who raised her, doesn't want her to come outside for decency's sake. So if there's someone who might ogle her, let him have patience.[8]

It remains for me to tell you that the author of this comedy is a very well-mannered man,[9] and that he would be troubled

---

[6] accusation: *carico*, elsewhere translated as "reproach" or "bad name."

[7] or "license": *licenzia*.

[8] ogle her: *la vagheggiare*: gaze longingly, cast an amorous glance.

patience: *pazienza*: calm endurance or forbearance of desire. Machiavelli here mimics a convention of Renaissance comedy—actually a continuation of an old Roman custom—by not showing the young virgin on stage. See Mera Flaumenhaft, "The Comic Remedy: Machiavelli's *Mandragola*," *Interpretation: A Journal of Political Philosophy*, vol. 7, no. 2 [1978].

[9] very well-mannered man: *uomo molto costumato*: an adherent of established customs or conventions.

indecency: *disonesta*. See note 3 above.

if, while seeing it performed, there should appear to you to be some indecency in it. He doesn't believe that there is any. However, if it should appear so to you, he excuses himself in this way: Comedies were discovered[10] in order to benefit and to delight the spectators. Truly it is a great benefit to any man, and especially to a youth, to know the avarice of an old man, the passion of a lover, the tricks[11] of a servant, the gluttony of a parasite, the misery of a pauper, the ambition of one who's rich, the flatteries of a whore, the untrustworthiness[12] of all men. Comedies are full of such examples, and all these things can be presented with very great decency. But if one wants to delight, it is necessary to move the spectators to laughter, and this cannot be done if one keeps to grave and severe speech. For the words that cause laughter are either silly or insulting[13] or amorous, and it is therefore necessary to portray characters who are silly, slanderous or in love. And so comedies that are full of these three kinds of speech are full of laughter, while those that lack them do not find anyone to laugh along with them.

Since, then, our author wants to delight and in some places to make the spectators laugh, yet has not brought silly characters into his comedy and refrains from speaking ill, he has been compelled to take recourse in characters in love and to accidents that arise in love. If there's anything in here that isn't decent, it will be said in such a way that the women will be able to listen to it without blushing. Be content, then, to lend us your kind ears, and if you satisfy us by listening, we will strive in performing to satisfy you.

---

[10] or "invented": *trovate*.

[11] tricks: *inganni* (sing. *inganno*): deception, artful cleverness. See the song at the conclusion of act IV.

[12] or "small faith": *poca fede*.

[13] insulting: *iniurioso*: also "harmful."

ACT ONE

Scene One
Palamede, Cleandro

PALAMEDE: Why are you leaving the house so early?

CLEANDRO: Where are you coming from so early?

PALAMEDE: From taking care of some of my business.

CLEANDRO: And I'm going to take care of some too, or, to say it better, to try to, for whether I can do it or not I'm not at all certain.

PALAMEDE: Is it a matter that can be spoken of?

CLEANDRO: I don't know, but I know well that it's a matter that can be accomplished with difficulty.

PALAMEDE: That's it! I'm going to get out of here, because I see how remaining in your company annoys you. And I've always avoided associating with you for just this reason, because I've always found you out of sorts and eccentric.[14]

CLEANDRO: Eccentric, no, but in love, yes.

PALAMEDE: You don't say! Well, you're sure setting my hat straight on my head![15]

CLEANDRO: My dear Palamede, you don't know half the masses.[16] I've always lived in despair, and I live so now more than ever.

PALAMEDE: How so?

---

[14] out of sorts: *mal disposto*: in a bad disposition.
eccentric: *fantastico*: someone given to fantasies and wild imaginings. See note 30 below.

[15] Sarcasm. Stage translation: "Well, I'm so glad you set me straight on that!"

[16] Stage translation: ". . . you don't know half of what needs to be known."

CLEANDRO: What I've concealed from you before I now want to make plain to you, now that I've been brought to the point where I need everyone's assistance.

PALAMEDE: If I stayed with you unwillingly before, I'll do so even more unwillingly now, because I've always understood that three sorts of men ought to be avoided: singers, old men and lovers. Because if you hang out with a singer and tell him about some of your business, when you believe that he's listening to you he belts out a *do, re, mi, fa, so, la* and gurgles a little song in his throat. If you're with an old man, he sticks his head into every church he finds and goes up to all the altars to mutter an Our Father. But the lover is worse than these two, because it's not enough that if you speak to him he's planting a vine, [17] but he fills your ears with complaints and with so many of his anxieties that you're forced to be moved to compassion. For if he hangs out with a street-walker, either she torments him excessively or she has him driven out of the house; there's always something to talk about. If he loves a good woman, [18] a thousand envies, a thousand jealousies, a thousand affronts disturb him— never does he lack cause for complaining. So, my dear Cleandro, I'll hang around with you for as long as you need me; otherwise, I'll run away from these complaints of yours.

CLEANDRO: I've kept this passion of mine hidden up until now for just these reasons: so that I wouldn't be fled from as annoying, or made fun of as ridiculous. Because I know that many, under a pretense of kindness, get you to talk with them and then later mock you behind your back. But since fortune has now brought me to a place where it seems to me that I have few remedies, I want to confer with you, partly

---

[17] A proverbial expression apparently meaning that one is too preoccupied with other activities to pay any attention (Guerri). Stage translation: ". . . he's too busy to listen, like a person tending to his vineyard . . ."

[18] good woman: *una donna da bene*: a gentlewoman, a woman of noble birth and good character.

in order to get it off my chest,[19] and also because, if I need your help, you can lend me a hand.

PALAMEDE: I'm prepared, since it's what you want, to listen to everything, and in this way to flee neither hardships nor dangers in order to help you.

CLEANDRO: I know it. I believe you know about the young girl we've raised here.

PALAMEDE: I've seen her. Where did she come from?

CLEANDRO: I'll tell you. When, twelve years ago in 1494, King Charles passed through Florence as he was going with a great army to the enterprise against the Kingdom,[20] there was billeted in our house a gentleman of Monsieur de Foix's company, named Beltramo of Guascogna. He was honored by my father and, because he was a good man,[21] he respected and honored our household; and whereas many made enemies of the Frenchmen they had in their houses, my father and he contracted a very great friendship.

PALAMEDE: You had greater luck than others, because those who were put into our house committed infinite evils against us.

CLEANDRO: I believe it! But it didn't happen that way to us. This Beltramo went from here with his king to Naples and, as you know, after Charles had vanquished that kingdom he was compelled to depart, because the Pope, the Emperor, the Venetians and the Duke of Milan allied themselves against him. So, with some of his men being left at Naples, with the rest he came from there towards Tuscany, and,

---

[19] get it off my chest: *sfogarmi*.

[20] The Kingdom: Naples. A reference to Charles VIII's unresisted invasion of Italy, which marked the beginning of a turbulent period in Italian and Florentine politics. The invasion and its aftermath are recounted by Machiavelli in verse in the *First Decennale*, a historical poem on Italian and Florentine affairs from 1494–1504. The events spoken of here, along with later indications that the action takes place during Carnival season (cf. II.3), allow us to fix the dramatic date of the play in January or February of 1506.

[21] good man: *uomo da bene*: a customary term for a gentleman.

having arrived at Siena, when he learned that the League had a very large army above the Taro in order to do battle with him as he descended the mountains, it appeared to him that he ought not to lose time in Tuscany. Therefore, not through Florence, but by way of Pisa and of Pontremoli, he passed into Lombardy. Beltramo, hearing the rumor of the enemy and being worried that—as in fact happened—he would have to go to battle[22] against them, and having among the plunder taken from Naples this young girl who was then five years old, beautiful in appearance and completely gentle,[23] he decided to remove her from the dangers, and through one of his servants he sent her to my father, begging him out of love for him to keep her until he could send for her at a more convenient time. He didn't send word as to whether she was of noble or ignoble birth;[24] he indicated to us only that she was named Clizia. My mother and my father, since they had no children other than myself, immediately fell in love with her . . .

PALAMEDE: You probably fell in love with her too!

CLEANDRO: Let me speak! . . . and they treated her as their own dear daughter. I, who was ten years old at the time, began to play with her as children do, and I conceived an extraordinary love for her, which constantly increased with age; so that, when she got to be twelve years old, my father and mother began to keep their eyes on my hands, such that if I even spoke with her the household went bottoms up. This restriction—since one always has a greater desire for that which is less permitted—redoubled my love, and has made, and does make, so much war against me that I live with more anxieties than if I were in Hell.

---

[22] go to battle: *fare la giornata*: literally "make the day."

[23] appearance: *aria*: also "air" or "bearing."
completely gentle: *tutta gentile*. The term can also mean "polite," "kind," "tender" or "of noble breeding."

[24] noble or ignoble birth: *nobile o ignobile*: that is, whether she was born to an aristocratic or a common family.

PALAMEDE: Beltramo, did he ever send for her?

CLEANDRO: We never heard anything of him. We believe that he died in the battle of the Taro.

PALAMEDE: So it must have been. But tell me, what are you going to do? Where are you with this? Do you want to take her as a wife, or do you want her as your mistress? What stands in your way, since you have her in your house? Can it really be that you have no remedy here?

CLEANDRO: I have to tell you other things that will be to my shame, but I want you to know everything.

PALAMEDE: Speak, then.

CLEANDRO: "And the wish comes upon me," she says,[25] "to laugh, but I hurt!"—My father has also fallen in love with her.

PALAMEDE: Nicomaco?

CLEANDRO: Nicomaco, yes.

PALAMEDE: Can it be, by God!

CLEANDRO: It can be, by God and Saints!

PALAMEDE: Oh, this is the finest affair I've ever heard of. And it ruins nothing except a household. How are you living together? What are you doing? What are you planning? Your mother, does she know about this?

CLEANDRO: My mother knows it, and the maids, and the servants—it's a public party, this affair of ours.

PALAMEDE: Tell me, in the end, where does the matter lie?

CLEANDRO: I'll tell you. My father, even if he weren't in love with her, would never grant her to me as a wife, because he's greedy[26] and she doesn't have a dowry. He's also worried that she might be of ignoble birth.[27] I, for my part, would

---

[25] A reference to some indeterminate, probably proverbial character.

[26] greedy: *avaro:* avaricious, acquisitive. Elsewhere Machiavelli notes that the term *avaro,* unlike *misero* (mean, miserly), denotes someone who desires to get something by violent means (cf. *The Prince,* xv).

[27] ignoble birth: *ignobile.*

take her as a wife, as a mistress, and in every way that I could have her. But we don't have to discuss[28] this now. I'll tell you only where we find ourselves.

PALAMEDE: I'd appreciate that.

CLEANDRO: As soon as my father fell in love with her, which must have been about a year ago, since he desired to satisfy this longing, which actually sends him into spasms, he thought that there would be no other remedy than to marry her off to someone who afterwards would share her in common with him, for to attempt to have her before she married must have seemed to him something impious and ugly. And not knowing where to turn, he selected as the most trustworthy[29] for this matter Pirro, our servant, and he managed this fantasy[30] of his so secretly that he was a hair away from realizing it before others became aware of it. But Sofronia, my mother, who a little earlier had perceived the love, discovered this plot, and with all industry, moved by jealousy and envy, is putting a hand to spoiling it. This she can't do any better than by sending into the field another groom and finding fault with the first; and she says that she wants to give her to Eustachio, our steward. And although Nicomaco has more authority, nevertheless my mother's astuteness,[31] along with the help of the rest of us—that we give to her without revealing ourselves too much—has kept the matter in suspense for several weeks. Yet Nicomaco is pressing us hard, and he has decided in spite of sea and wind to bring about this marriage today: he wants him to

---

[28] or "reason about": ragionare.

[29] or "faithful": fidato.

[30] fantasy: fantasia. The meaning of this word is impossible to convey by means of a single English equivalent, since it ranges from thought, mind or idea, to imagination, whim or fantasy, to sexual longing or desire. It occurs four times in the play, and with one exception (III.2: "mind") it will be translated simply as "fantasy." See also note 14 above.

[31] astuteness: astuzia: cleverness. Cf. the opening paragraph of chapter xviii of The Prince.

marry her this evening, and he has rented for him that little house where our neighbor Damone lives. And he says that he wants to buy it for him, to furnish it with household goods, to open a shop for him and to make him rich.

PALAMEDE: What does it matter to you if Pirro has her rather than Eustachio?

CLEANDRO: What do you mean, what does it matter to me? This Pirro is the biggest scoundrel there is in Florence. Besides having bargained with my father for her, he's a man who has always hated me, so that I would sooner want the devil in Hell to have her. I wrote to the steward yesterday, telling him that he should come to Florence. I'm amazed that he didn't come yesterday evening. I'm going to stay here to see if I can spot him turning up. What are you going to do?

PALAMEDE: I'm going to take care of some of my business.

CLEANDRO: Go, then. In good time.

PALAMEDE: Farewell. Delay it as best you can, and if you want something, say so.

Scene Two
Cleandro alone

Truly, he who said that the lover and the soldier are alike spoke the truth. The captain wants his soldiers young; women want their lovers not to be old. It's an ugly thing to see an old man as a soldier; it's a very ugly thing to see him in love. Soldiers fear the anger of their captain, lovers not less that of their women. Soldiers sleep on the ground in the open air, lovers on low walls. Soldiers pursue to the death their enemies, lovers their rivals. Soldiers, through the dark of night, in the most frigid winter, go through the mud, exposed to water and wind, to accomplish an enterprise that might enable them to acquire victory; lovers along similar paths, and with similar and greater hardships, seek to acquire their beloved. Equally in military affairs and in love there is a necessity for secrecy, trust[32] and spiritedness: the dangers are equal, and the outcome most of the time is similar. The soldier dies in a ditch, the lover dies in desperation. I'm worried that it may turn out this way for me. I have the woman at home, I see her as much as I want, I dine with her all the time! This, I believe, is a source of greater pain for me, for the nearer a man is to one of his desires, the more he desires it, and if he doesn't have it, he feels a greater pain. For now, I need to plan to upset this wedding. Later, new accidents[33] may bring me new counsels and new fortunes. Is it possible that Eustachio didn't come from the country? I wrote to him that he should be here by yesterday evening! But I see him peeking out there, from that corner. Eustachio! Hey, Eustachio!

Scene Three
Eustachio, Cleandro

EUSTACHIO: Who's calling me? Oh, Cleandro!

CLEANDRO: Why have you waited so long to show up?

EUSTACHIO: I came yesterday evening, but I didn't reveal myself, because a little while before I had your letter I had one from Nicomaco that directed me to do a mountain of business; I didn't want to run into him unless I saw you first.

CLEANDRO: You've done well. I sent for you because Nicomaco is hastening this wedding of Pirro, which, as you know, is something that doesn't please my mother; because, since a gift of this young girl must be made to one of our men, she would like her to be given to whoever deserves her most. And in truth your circumstances are quite different from Pirro's, for, to say it here between us, he's a wretch.

EUSTACHIO: I thank you. And truly, I didn't have it in my head to take a wife, but since you and the madonna want it, I want

---

[32] or "faith": *fede*.

[33] accidents: *accidenti*. Cf. note 4 above.

it too, I do. It's true that I wouldn't want to make Nicomaco my enemy, since, in the end, he is the master.[34]

CLEANDRO: Don't worry, for my mother and I won't fail you, and we'll pull you out of every danger. I'd very much like for you to fix yourself up a bit. You have this cloak that's falling off your back, this dusty cap, a shaggy beard. Go to the barber, wash your face, dust off these clothes, so that Clizia won't reject you as a swine.

EUSTACHIO: I'm not likely to make myself pretty.

CLEANDRO: Go, do what I tell you, and then go into that neighboring church and wait for me there. I'm going into the house to see what the old man is planning.

Song[35]

He who makes no test, Love,
of your great power, hopes in vain
ever to bear true witness[36] to
what may be heaven's highest worth;
nor does he know how one can at the same time
  live and die,
how one can pursue harm and flee good,
how one can love oneself
less than others, how often
fear and hope make hearts freeze and melt;
nor does he know how men and gods in equal measure
dread the arms with which you're armed.

---

[34] master: *padrone.*

[35] The same song appears at the end of act I of Machiavelli's *The Mandragola.*

[36] bear true witness: *fare fede vera.*

ACT TWO

Scene One
Nicomaco alone

Good Lord, what do I have around my eyes this morning? I seem to have flashes that don't let me see the light, yet last evening I could have seen the hair in an egg. Could it be that I drank too much? Maybe so. Oh God, this old age comes with every affliction! But, I'm not yet so old that I can't break a lance with Clizia. Is it really possible that I'm in love in this way? And, what's worse, my wife is alert to it, and she suspects why I want to give the girl to Pirro. In short, my furrow doesn't run straight. Still, I have to try to get my victory. Pirro! Hey Pirro! Come down, come outside!

Scene Two
Pirro, Nicomaco

PIRRO: Here I am!

NICOMACO: Pirro, I want you to take a wife this evening, at all costs.

PIRRO: I'll take her now.

NICOMACO: Slow up a bit! "One thing at a time," as Mirra says.[37] Things also have to be done in such a way that the household doesn't get turned bottoms up. You see, my wife isn't content with this, Eustachio also wants her for himself, and it seems to me that Cleandro favors him—both God and the devil are

---

[37] The Italian is a proverbial saying (*A cosa, a cosa*). Mirra (elsewhere one finds Mirrancia) was an indeterminate proverbial figure to whom these and other sayings were attributed (Guerri).

15

turned against us. But still, stay strong in the faith that you'll have her, and don't worry, since I'll be worth all of them together. For, if it comes to the worst, I'll give her to you in spite of them, and whoever wants to get upset, let him get upset.

PIRRO: In the name of God, tell me what you want me to do.

NICOMACO: Don't stray from here, so that if I want you, you can be quick about it.

PIRRO: I'll do it. But I forgot to tell you something.

NICOMACO: What?

PIRRO: Eustachio is in Florence.

NICOMACO: What! In Florence? Who told you this?

PIRRO: Sir Ambrugio, our neighbor in the country. He told me that he came inside the gate with him yesterday evening.

NICOMACO: What! Yesterday evening? Where did he stay last night?

PIRRO: Who knows?

NICOMACO: So be it; all in good time. Go ahead, do what I told you.

[*Exit Pirro*]

Sofronia must have sent for Eustachio, and this scoundrel has attached greater importance to her letter than to my own, in which I wrote to him to do a thousand things that'll bring me to ruin if they aren't done. In the name of God, I'll pay him back for this! At least I know where he is and what he's doing. But here's Sofronia coming out of the house.

Scene Three
Sofronia, Nicomaco

SOFRONIA: [*Aside*] I've shut Clizia up in her room with Doria. I need to defend this girl from my son, from my husband and from the servants: everyone has set up camp around her.

NICOMACO: Where are you going?

SOFRONIA: To mass.

NICOMACO: And it's only Carnival.[38] Think what you'll do for Lent!

SOFRONIA: I believe that one ought to do good all the time, and it's so much more welcome for it to be done on those occasions when others are doing evil. But it seems to me that as for our doing good, we're setting out from a wicked place!

NICOMACO: What? What would you like us to do?

SOFRONIA: For us not to think about chatting idly, and, since we have a very good and beautiful girl at home, whom we've labored to raise, to think about not throwing her away. Whereas every man praised us before, now every man will find fault with us, seeing us give her away to a glutton without a brain who doesn't know how to do anything except a little shaving, which not even a fly could live on!

NICOMACO: My dear Sofronia, you're mistaken. He's a young man with good looks, and if he doesn't know [much], he's suited to learn, and he's fond of her.[39] These are three great qualities in a husband: youth, beauty and love. It doesn't seem to me that one could do more here, or that one finds such matches at every doorstep. If he lacks property, you know that property comes and goes, and he's one of those who's suited to make it come. And I won't abandon him, because I intend, to tell you the truth, to buy him that house that I'm presently renting from Damone our neighbor and to fill it up with household goods. And, what's more, even if it costs me four hundred florins, to set him up . . .

---

[38] Carnival (from the Latin *carnem levare*, lit. "to remove flesh"), a time of feasting, pageantry and celebration that likely has roots in the pagan rites of antiquity, precedes the fast of Lent. A counterpart in America is the Mardi Gras celebration that occurs each March in New Orleans. As the sequel suggests, it is regularly an occasion for indecent behavior, moral transgression and excesses of many kinds, and is therefore also a time for the pious to pray and to serve penance for offenses against the Divine Law.

[39] fond of: *vuol bene.*

SOFRONIA: Ha, ha, ha!

NICOMACO: You're laughing?

SOFRONIA: Who wouldn't laugh?

NICOMACO: Yes, just what are you trying to say? . . . to set him up in a shop, I won't pay any attention to the expense.

SOFRONIA: Is it really possible that you intend with this strange match to take from your son more than is fitting and to give to that other more than he deserves? I don't know what to say. I worry that there may be something else here, underneath it all.

NICOMACO: What do you suppose there could be?

SOFRONIA: If there were someone here who didn't know, I'd tell him. But since you know it, I won't tell you about it.

NICOMACO: What do I know?

SOFRONIA: Let's leave this alone! What moves you to give her to him? With this dowry, or even less, couldn't we marry her better?

NICOMACO: Yes, I believe so. Nevertheless, I'm moved by the love that I have for both of them. For, since I raised both of them, I think I ought to benefit both of them.

SOFRONIA: But if this is what moves you, haven't you also raised Eustachio, your steward?

NICOMACO: Yes, I have. But do you really want us to give her to that one, who has no noble breeding[40] whatsoever and is accustomed to being in the country with the cattle and sheep? Oh! If we gave her to him, she'd die of grief.

SOFRONIA: And with Pirro she'll die of hunger. Let me remind you that the noble breeding of men consists in having some virtue,[41] knowing how to do something, as Eustachio knows,

---

[40] noble breeding: *gentilezza*: gentility, gentlemanliness.

[41] virtue: *virtú*. This is one of two occurrences in the play of this word, so prominent and important in Machiavelli's writings on politics (cf. the song at the conclusion of act II). Its precise meaning for Machiavelli is difficult to determine, and this ambiguity is almost certainly intentional: sometimes he uses the term to indicate

who's accustomed to business in the markets, to managing the household, to caring for the affairs of others and himself, and is a man who could live in water[42]—so much so that, as you know, he has a good bit of capital. Pirro, on the other hand, is never anywhere but in the taverns, at the gambling houses; he's a slacker who would die of hunger in Altopascio.[43]

NICOMACO: Didn't I tell you what I intend to give to him?

SOFRONIA: And didn't I answer you that you'd be throwing it away? I'll tell you this in conclusion, Nicomaco: You've spent money to feed her, and I've worked hard to raise her! And since I had a part in this, I also want to know how these matters are to proceed, or else I'll speak so much ill and stir up so many scandals that you'll find yourself in a bad condition, and I don't know how you'll show your face. Go, discuss[44] these things with your mask on![45]

NICOMACO: What are you saying to me? Are you crazy? Now you make me want to give her to him at all costs. And on account of this love, I want him to marry her this evening, and he will marry her, even if your eyes gush.

---

moral excellence or decency, at other times he employs it in the older Roman sense of courage or a general manliness of spirit (cf. the Latin *vir*, "man"), and on other occasions he uses it in a novel and radical way to refer to a constellation of qualities, of both intellect and spirit, that are conducive to acquisition and mastery, irrespective of the decency or manliness of the actions that yield this success. For an illustration of this deliberate ambiguity in Machiavelli's use of *virtú*, consider his discussion of the Sicilian tyrant Agathocles in chapter viii of *The Prince* (trans. Harvey C. Mansfield, Jr., [University of Chicago Press, 1985]).

[42] "could live in water": that is, he is so resourceful that he could survive and prosper even in a natural environment that is inhospitable to human life.

[43] The Altopascio, an area near the city of Lucca in the Tuscan region of central Italy, contains very fertile farmland. Hence, stage translation: ". . . who would die of starvation in the fertile farmland in the Altopascio."

[44] or "reason about": *ragiona*.

[45] Likely referring to the masquerades that took place at Carnival time (cf. III.1) and the indecency that such anonymity encouraged and facilitated.

SOFRONIA: Either he'll marry her, or he won't marry her.

NICOMACO: Threaten me with gossip, will you! Well, watch out that I don't talk. Maybe you believe that I'm blind and that I don't recognize this little juggling game of yours? I certainly knew that mothers are fond of their sons, but I didn't believe they'd be willing to take a hand in their indecency.

SOFRONIA: What do you mean? What's indecent?

NICOMACO: Come now, don't make me say it! You know and I know. Each of us knows how far off Saint Biagio's day is.[46] By your faith, let's come to an agreement on these matters, because if we get into this silliness we'll become a farce[47] for the people.

SOFRONIA: Enter into whatever silliness you want. This girl won't be thrown away, or else I'll turn not only our household bottoms up, but all of Florence too.

NICOMACO: Sofronia, Sofronia. Whoever gave you this name wasn't dreaming! You're a *soffiona*, and you're full of wind.[48]

SOFRONIA: In the name of God, I want to go to mass! We'll see each other again.

NICOMACO: Listen a bit. Is there some way to put a cap on this matter, so that we won't make ourselves look crazy?

SOFRONIA: Not crazy, but wicked,[49] yes indeed.

NICOMACO: There are so many good men in this city, we have so many relatives, and there are so many good clerics! Let's

---

[46] Saint Biagio: Saint Blaise or Blasius, reputedly a physician prior to becoming a bishop in Armenia, is believed to have suffered martyrdom at the beginning of the fourth century. In the Roman Church, the feast of Saint Blasius was moved one day to February 3, so as not to conflict with Candlemas on February 2 (Guerri). Stage translation: "Each of us knows exactly when Saint Blaise's day is. Neither of us was born yesterday."

[47] farce: *favola*: a pleasing or comedic tale, like the *Clizia* itself.

[48] *soffiona*: a bellows. Stage translation: "You were named after the *soffiona*, the bellows, and you blow a lot of hot air."

[49] wicked: *tristo*.

go and ask them about this matter that we don't agree on, and in this way either you or I will be freed from error.

SOFRONIA: Why do we want to start advertising this craziness of ours?

NICOMACO: If we don't want to choose either friends or relatives, let's choose a cleric, and it won't be advertised, since we'll submit the matter to him in confession.

SOFRONIA: To whom could we go?

NICOMACO: We couldn't go to anyone other than friar Timoteo, who is the confessor of our household and a little saint, and who has already accomplished a miracle.

SOFRONIA: Which?

NICOMACO: What do you mean, which? Don't you know that through his prayers Madonna Lucrezia, wife of Messer Nicia Calfucci, who was sterile, got pregnant?[50]

SOFRONIA: Some great miracle, a friar making a woman pregnant! It would be a miracle if a nun had made her pregnant!

NICOMACO: Is it possible that you might at some point stop blocking my way with this chattering.

SOFRONIA: I want to go to mass, and I don't want to submit my affairs to anyone.

NICOMACO: Well then, go, and I'll wait for you at home.

[*Exit Sofronia*]

I believe it's good for me not to stray too far, lest they carry Clizia off somewhere.

Scene Four
Sofronia alone

Whoever knew Nicomaco a year ago and associated with him now would be amazed at him when considering the great

---

[50] An allusion to the plot and characters of Machiavelli's play *The Mandragola*.

change that's come over him. Because he was accustomed to being a grave, stable and respectful man. He spent his time honorably. He got up early in the morning, heard his mass, provided for the day's food. Then, if he had some business in the public square, at the market, with the magistrates, he did it; if not, either he met with some citizen for honorable discussions[51] or he retired to his study at home, where he balanced his ledger and put his accounts in order. Later he dined peacefully with his company and, having dined, held discussions[52] with his son, offered him counsel, gave him to understand men and, by means of some ancient and modern examples, taught him how to live. Later he went outside and spent the entire day either in business or in grave and decent pastimes. When evening came, the Ave Maria always found him at home.[53] He sat with us for a little while by the fire if it was winter, and then he went into his study to look over his business. At nine o'clock[54] he had a cheerful supper. This arrangement[55] of his life was an example to everyone else in the household, and everyone was ashamed not to imitate him. And so matters proceeded in this way, orderly and cheerful.

But after he entered into this fantasy[56] concerning the girl, his business was neglected, his farms were laid waste, his business dealings went to ruin. He shouted constantly, without knowing why; he went in and out of the house a thousand times a day without knowing what he was going to do; he never returned at an hour when he could dine or have supper on time. If you spoke to him, either he didn't answer you, or he answered you but not to the point. And the servants, seeing

---

[51] or "reasonings": *ragionamenti.*

[52] or "reasoned": *ragionava.*

[53] Ave Maria: the Hail Mary, a prayer said as part of the rosary. Stage translation: ". . . he was always at home to say the evening prayer."

[54] The text reads "at three o'clock" (*a tre ore*), according to the old Italian custom of counting the hours from sunset, beginning at six o'clock in the evening.

[55] arrangement: *ordine*: ordering.

[56] *fantasia.* See note 30 above.

this, made fun of him, and his son cast aside his reverence. Everyone acted as he wished. In short, no one worried about doing what he saw him doing. In light of all of this, I'm worried that if God doesn't provide a remedy for us, this poor household will come to ruin. So I want to go to mass and commend myself to God as much as I can.

I see Eustachio and Pirro, quarreling. What fine husbands are being readied for Clizia!

Scene Five
Pirro, Eustachio

PIRRO: What're you doing in Florence, you wretched thing?

EUSTACHIO: I don't have to tell you.

PIRRO: You're so decked out, you look to me like a freshly cleaned toilet.

EUSTACHIO: You have such a little brain, I'm amazed the boys don't throw stones at your back.

PIRRO: Soon we'll see who has more of a brain, you or I.

EUSTACHIO: Pray to God that the master lives on, or else you'll become a beggar one day.

PIRRO: Have you seen Nicomaco?

EUSTACHIO: Why do you want to know whether I've seen him or not?

PIRRO: It'll mean a good deal to you to know it, because unless he changes his mind, if you don't go back to the country on your own he'll have the police carry you there.

EUSTACHIO: This bothers you quite a lot, my being in Florence!

PIRRO: It'll bother others more than me.

EUSTACHIO: Then leave thinking about it to others.

PIRRO: Still, the flesh pulls.[57]

---

[57] This saying also appears in act III, scene 3 of *The Mandragola*, where it indicates a longing for sexual intimacy. Its usage here is odd: perhaps Pirro means to say that his desire to have Clizia causes him also to be bothered about Eustachio's presence in Florence.

EUSTACHIO: You look on and grin.

PIRRO: I'm looking at what a fine husband you'll be.

EUSTACHIO: Well now, do you know what I have to say?—"And even the Duke built walls!"[58]—But if she takes you, she'll have jumped on the garden walls.[59] How much better it would be if Nicomaco were to drown her in his well! That way the poor thing would at least die all at once.

PIRRO: Heh, you lazy hick, perfumed in dung!

[*To audience*]

Does he think he has the flesh to sleep beside such a delicate girl?

EUSTACHIO: She'll have fine flesh with you! Because, if her wretched luck gives her to you, either she'll become a whore within a year or she'll die of grief. But you'll be satisfied with the first, because when it comes to being a contented cuckold,[60] you're just the guy.

PIRRO: Let's let this go, and let's each of us sharpen his little tool. We'll see who'll come out better. I'm going into the house, so that I don't bash your head in.

EUSTACHIO: And I'm going back into the church.

PIRRO: You'd do well not to leave your sanctuary.[61]

---

[58] In the context, it appears to mean that it is not shameful for anyone to do hard labor (Guerri).

[59] Either to beg for alms (Guerri), or alternatively, as the sequel suggests, to prostitute herself.

[60] contented cuckold: *uno becco pappataci*: a fed and quieted cuckold.

[61] Referring to the immunity to civil arrest usually accorded to those who take refuge in a church. Pirro is reiterating his earlier threat that Nicomaco will have Eustachio arrested and returned to the countryside against his will.

Song

As beautiful as love is in a youthful heart,
equally unseemly is it
in one who has passed the flower of his years.
Love has virtues equal to one's age:
in years of bloom it receives much honor,
but in older age it's worth little, or nothing at all.
So, you old lovers, it would be best
to leave this enterprise to ardent youths
who, being ready for more demanding work,
can pay its lord a greater honor.

ACT THREE

Scene One
Nicomaco, Cleandro

NICOMACO: Cleandro, oh Cleandro!

CLEANDRO: Sir!

NICOMACO: Come down, come down, I say. What are you doing that keeps you in the house so much? Aren't you ashamed? You're giving a bad name[62] to that girl! On these days of Carnival it's customary for young men like you to amuse themselves by looking at the masks or going to play soccer. You're one of those men who doesn't know how to do anything, and you seem to me to be neither dead nor alive.

CLEANDRO: I don't enjoy these things, and they've never given me any enjoyment, but it pleases me more to remain alone than to be with that kind of company. And now I stay home so much more willingly because I see that you're here, for if you want anything I'll be able to do it.

NICOMACO: [*Aside*] Heh, look at how he makes excuses.[63]

[To Cleandro]

You're a good son! But I don't need to have you trailing behind me all day long. I keep two servants and a steward so that I won't have to order you around.

CLEANDRO: In the name of God! Really, it isn't that what I do isn't done for the good.

---

[62] bad name: *carico*: bad reputation, grounds for reproach or accusation.

[63] look . . . excuses: *guarda dove la l'aveva*: lit. "look where he had it": look where he found his good reasons (ironic), hence, look at the excuses he turns to (Blasucci).

26

NICOMACO: I don't know why you do it. But I know for sure that your mother is a crazy woman and that she'll bring this house to ruin. You'd better repair it.

CLEANDRO: Either she will, or others.

NICOMACO: Which others?

CLEANDRO: I don't know.

NICOMACO: It seems clear to me that you don't know it. But what do you have to say about these matters[64] concerning Clizia?

CLEANDRO: [*Aside*] See how we end up here!

NICOMACO: What did you say? Speak up, so that I can understand you.

CLEANDRO: I said that I don't know what to say about this.

NICOMACO: Doesn't it seem to you that your mother is choosing a crab[65] by not wanting Clizia to become Pirro's wife?

CLEANDRO: I don't know anything about it.

NICOMACO: I know it clearly. You've taken her side, and there's something else lurking here beneath your pleasing tales.[66] Do you really think that she would fare well with Eustachio?

CLEANDRO: I don't know about it and I don't understand any of this.

NICOMACO: What the devil do you understand?

CLEANDRO: Not this.

NICOMACO: Yet you understood how to make Eustachio come to Florence and how to hide him away so that I wouldn't see him, and how to set a snare for me in order to spoil this wedding. But I'll lock both of you up in the Stinche,[67] and

---

[64] these matters: *questi casi*.

[65] choosing a crab: *pigliare un granchio*. Stage translation: ". . . making a big mistake."

[66] pleasing tales: *favole*. See note 47 above.

[67] Stinche: a prison in Florence. Machiavelli recounts the origin of its name in *Florentine Histories*, II.22. Stage translation: ". . . the Stinche prison."

I'll return the dowry to Sofronia and send her on her way.
For I intend to be the lord of my household, and let everyone
uncork his ears to that! And I intend for this wedding to take
place this evening; or else, if I have no other remedy, I'll set
fire to this house. I'll wait for your mother here, to see if I
can come to some agreement with her. But if I can't, at all
costs I want my honor here, and I don't intend for the
goslings to lead the geese to drink. Go then, if you desire
your well-being and peace for the household, and beg your
mother to do things my way. You'll find her at church, and
I'll wait for you and her here at home. And if you see that
scoundrel Eustachio tell him to come to me, and that if he
doesn't his affairs[68] won't ever go well!

CLEANDRO: I'm going.

Scene Two
Cleandro alone

Oh, the misery of the lover! With how many anxieties I pass
my time! I know well that whoever loves a beautiful thing like
Clizia has many rivals who give him infinite sorrows. But I've
never heard it happen that someone had his own father as a
rival. Whereas many young men have found some remedy from
their fathers, I find in mine the very foundation and cause of
my harm. And while my mother favors me, she doesn't do it
in order to favor me but in order to disfavor her husband's
enterprise. And so I can't reveal myself boldly in this matter,
because immediately she would believe that I've made the same
pact with Eustachio that my father has made with Pirro; and
if she believed this, moved by her conscience she would let the
water run downhill[69] and wouldn't work for this end any more.
Then I'd be completely undone, and I'd be so displeased by it
that I don't believe I could live any longer.

---

[68] affairs: *casi.*

[69] Stage translation: ". . . would wash her hands of the whole afffair."

I see my mother coming out of the church. I want to speak with her to find out what's on her mind,[70] to see what remedies she's preparing for the old man's plans.

Scene Three
Cleandro, Sofronia

CLEANDRO: God save you, dear mother!

SOFRONIA: Oh Cleandro, are you coming from home?

CLEANDRO: Yes, Madonna.

SOFRONIA: Have you been there the whole time since I left you there?

CLEANDRO: I have.

SOFRONIA: Nicomaco, is he there?

CLEANDRO: He's in the house, and no matter what happens he isn't going out.

SOFRONIA: Let him behave so, in the name of God! The glutton thinks one thing, the innkeeper another.[71] Has he said anything?

CLEANDRO: A mountain of foul abuses, and I think the devil has got into him. He wants to put Eustachio and me in the Stinche, he wants to return the dowry to you and throw you out, and he's threatening nothing less than to set the house on fire. He has directed me to find you and persuade you to consent to this wedding; otherwise, things won't go well for you.

SOFRONIA: What do you have to say about this?

CLEANDRO: I say what you say. For I love Clizia like a sister, and it would pain me to my soul if she ended up in Pirro's hands.

---

[70] mind: *fantasia*. See note 30 above.

[71] The glutton . . . another: equivalent to "He reckons without the host," that is, he neglects the opposition.

SOFRONIA: I don't know how you love her. But I tell you this plainly, that if I believed that I'd be taking her out of Nicomaco's hands just to put her into yours, I wouldn't intervene in this. But I think that Eustachio would like her for himself, and that the love you have for her can be canceled out by means of your spouse (whom we're going to give to you very soon).

CLEANDRO: Good thinking. And really, I beg you to do everything to ensure that this wedding not take place. And if this can't be accomplished in any other way than by giving her to Eustachio, then give her to him; but if it can, it would be better, I think, to leave her as she is. For she's still young and time's not flying by. The heavens could cause her to find her family, and if they're noble, they wouldn't be much obliged to you upon finding that you've married her off to a servant or a peasant.

SOFRONIA: You're right. I've thought of this too, but the old man's violent passion[72] scares me. Nonetheless, I have so many things revolving in my head, and I believe that there's one to spoil his every plan. I want to go back to the house, because I see Nicomaco hovering around the door. Go to the church and tell Eustachio to come to the house and not to be afraid of anything.

CLEANDRO: I'll do this.

Scene Four
Nicomaco, Sofronia

NICOMACO: [*Aside*] I see my wife returning. I want to banter with her a bit, to see if good words can help me.

[*To Sofronia*]
Oh my dear girl, are you really going to stay so sad when you see the object of your hope?[73] Stay with me a bit.

---

[72] violent passion: *rabbia*.

[73] object of your hope: *la tua speranza*. Stage translation: ". . . the man of your dreams."

SOFRONIA: Let me go.

NICOMACO: Stand still for me, I say.

SOFRONIA: I don't want to. You look like you're stewed.[74]

NICOMACO: I'll come behind you.

SOFRONIA: Are you crazy?

NICOMACO: Crazy, just because I'm too fond of you?[75]

SOFRONIA: I don't want you to be fond of me.

NICOMACO: This can't be!

SOFRONIA: You're killing me! Oh, how disgusting!

NICOMACO: I'd rather you told the truth.

SOFRONIA: I believe it.

NICOMACO: Ah! Look at me a bit, my love.

SOFRONIA: I'm looking at you, and smelling you too. You smell good! Well, well, you're starting to get to me![76]

NICOMACO: [Aside] Damn! She's noticed it! Cursed be that good-for-nothing who brought this to me!

SOFRONIA: These fragrances that you smell of, where did they come from, you crazy old man?

NICOMACO: Someone who was selling them passed by here just now. I handled them, and some of the fragrance remained on me.

SOFRONIA: [Aside] He's already come up with a lie. Didn't I say so?

[To Nicomaco]

Aren't you ashamed of what you've been doing here this past year? You constantly hang out with six young men, you go to the taverns, you frequent brothels and gambling houses, you spend without moderation.[77] Some fine example you're setting for your son! Give a wife to these worthy men!

NICOMACO: Ah, my dear wife, don't accuse me of all these evils all at once! Keep something in reserve for tomorrow! But isn't it reasonable for you to do things my way rather than I yours?

SOFRONIA: Yes, when it comes to decent things.

NICOMACO: Isn't it decent to marry off a girl?

SOFRONIA: Yes, when she's married well.

NICOMACO: And won't she be well off with Pirro?

SOFRONIA: No.

NICOMACO: Why not?

SOFRONIA: For the reasons I've told you on other occasions.

NICOMACO: I understand more about these matters than you do. But what if I dealt with Eustachio in such a way that he didn't want her?

SOFRONIA: And what if I dealt with Pirro in such a way that he didn't want her either.

NICOMACO: From now on, let's each put this to the test, and whoever persuades his man will be victorious.

SOFRONIA: I'm content with this. I'm going into the house to speak to Pirro, and you'll speak with Eustachio, whom I see coming out of the church.

NICOMACO: Let it be done.

Scene Five
Eustachio, Nicomaco

EUSTACHIO: [*Aside*] Since Cleandro told me to go into the house and not to worry, I want to pluck up my courage and go there.

---

[77] without moderation: *sanza modo*.

NICOMACO: [*Aside*] I have a page full of abuses that I want to heap on this scoundrel, but I can't, since I have to plead with him.

[*To Eustachio*]

Hey, Eustachio!

EUSTACHIO: Oh, Master!

NICOMACO: When did you get to Florence?

EUSTACHIO: Yesterday evening.

NICOMACO: You've waited so long to let yourself be seen. Where have you been for so long?

EUSTACHIO: I'll tell you. Yesterday morning I began to feel sick: I had a headache and a pain in my groin, and I thought I had a fever, and since there's a suspicion of plague in these times, I was very worried. Yesterday evening I came to Florence and I stayed at an inn; I didn't want to show myself because I didn't want to make you or your family sick, if indeed it was what I thought it was. But, grace of God, everything has gone away and I feel fine.

NICOMACO: [*Aside*] I need to make it look like I believe him.

[*To Eustachio*]

You did well! Are you completely cured now?

EUSTACHIO: Yes sir.

NICOMACO: [*Aside*] Not of wickedness.

[*To Eustachio*]

I'm glad you're here. You know about this dispute between myself and my wife over giving Clizia a husband. She wants to give her to you, and I'd like to give her to Pirro.

EUSTACHIO: So then, you're fonder of Pirro than of me?

NICOMACO: Not at all. I'm fonder of you than of him. Listen a bit. What do you want with a wife? You're already thirty-eight years old, and a young girl won't be good for you, and it's reasonable that after she's been with you for some months she'll search out someone younger than you, and you'll live in despair. Then I won't be able to rely on you any longer: you'll lose your employment, you'll become poor, and you'll have to go begging, both of you.

EUSTACHIO: In this city whoever has a beautiful wife can't ever be poor. With a fireplace and a wife you can be liberal with everyone, because the more you give them away the more is left over for you.

NICOMACO: So then, do you want to get married in order to displease me?

EUSTACHIO: Not at all. I'm going to do it to please me!

NICOMACO: Be off now, go into the house. [*Aside*] I was crazy to think I'd get an agreeable response from this lout.

[*To Eustachio*]

I'll change my course with you. Prepare to turn in the accounts to me, and to go with God. And consider yourself the greatest enemy I have, and know that I'll do the worst to you that I can.

EUSTACHIO: This doesn't trouble me at all, provided that I get Clizia.

NICOMACO: You'll get the gallows!

Scene Six
Pirro, Nicomaco

PIRRO: [*Exiting the house, shouting over his shoulder*] Before I'd do what you ask, I'd let myself be skinned alive!

NICOMACO: [*Aside*] It's going well! Pirro remains trustworthy.[78]

[*To Pirro*]

What's the matter? Against whom are you battling, Pirro?

PIRRO: I'm battling against the same one that you're always battling against.

NICOMACO: What did she say? What did she want?

PIRRO: She begged me not to take Clizia for my wife.

---

[78] *stare nella fede*: remains faithful.

NICOMACO: What did you tell her?

PIRRO: That I would sooner be killed than reject her.

NICOMACO: You spoke well.

PIRRO: Maybe I spoke well, but I'm worried that I may have acted badly, because I made enemies of your wife, your son and all the others of the household.

NICOMACO: Why does that matter to you? Stand well with Christ, and scoff at the saints!

PIRRO: Yes, but if you should die, the saints would treat me very badly.

NICOMACO: Don't worry. I'll give you such a share[79] that the saints won't be able to give you much trouble. And if in fact they want to, the magistrates and the laws will defend you, provided I'm able,[80] by means of your aid, to sleep with Clizia.

PIRRO: I'm worried that you won't be able to, when I see how inflamed your wife is against you.

NICOMACO: I've decided that it would be good, in order to get out of this insanity once and for all, to choose by lot who'll get Clizia. My wife couldn't be at odds with this.

PIRRO: What if the lot goes against you?

NICOMACO: I have hope in God that this won't happen.

PIRRO: [*Aside*] What a crazy old man! He wants God to take a hand in his indecency!

[*To Nicomaco*]
I believe that if God intervenes in such matters, Sofronia too may have some hope in God.

NICOMACO: Let her hope! And if in fact the lot goes against me, I've thought of a remedy. Go, call her, and tell her to come outside with Eustachio.

---

[79] share: that is, of inheritance.

[80] I'm able: *abbio facultà.*

PIRRO: [*Calling inside*] Sofronia, you and Eustachio come to the master.

Scene Seven
Sofronia, Eustachio, Nicomaco, Pirro

SOFRONIA: Here I am. What news is there?

NICOMACO: We need to resolve this matter. You see, since they can't agree, it's fitting that we reach an agreement.

SOFRONIA: This passion[81] of yours is extraordinary. What can't be done today can be done tomorrow.

NICOMACO: I want to do it today.

SOFRONIA: Let it be done quickly, then. Here are the two competitors. How do you want to do this?

NICOMACO: I've come up with the thought that, since we can't agree with each other, we should submit the matter to fortune.

SOFRONIA: How so, to fortune?

NICOMACO: In one bag we'll place their names, and in another the name of Clizia and a blank ballot. First we'll draw one of their names, and whoever receives Clizia, let him have her, and let the other have patience.[82] What do you think? Aren't you going to answer?

SOFRONIA: All right, I'm content with this.

EUSTACHIO: Watch what you're doing.

SOFRONIA: I'm watching, and I know what I'm doing. Go into the house, write the ballots and fetch two bags, because I want to get out of this distress, or else I'll enter into a still greater one.

EUSTACHIO: I'm going.

---

[81] passion: *furia*.

[82] patience: *pazienza*. See note 8 above.

[*Exit*]

NICOMACO: In this way we'll come to an agreement. Pray to God, Pirro, for yourself.

PIRRO: For you!

NICOMACO: [*Aside*] You're right to say for me. It'll be a great consolation for me if you get her.

[*Enter Eustachio*]

EUSTACHIO: Here are the bags and the lots.

NICOMACO: Give them here. What does this one say? "Clizia." And this other? It's blank. Good. Put them in this bag here. What does this one say? "Eustachio." And the other? "Pirro." Fold them up and put them in the other one. Close them up, and you keep your eyes on them, Pirro, so that nothing happens as if under a hood.[83] After all, there's someone here who knows how to play the *macatelle*![84]

SOFRONIA: Distrustful men aren't good.

NICOMACO: Those are just words! You know that in fact it's the one who doesn't trust[85] who isn't deceived. Whom do we want to make the drawing?

SOFRONIA: Have whomever you want make the drawing.

NICOMACO: Come here, boy.

SOFRONIA: He should be a virgin.

NICOMACO: Virgin or not, I haven't held my hands there.[86] Draw a ballot from this bag, after I've said some prayers:—O Saint

---

[83] hood: *caperuccia*: the hood of a cape (Blasucci). Stage translation: ". . . Pirro, to make sure that nothing goes unseen, as if hidden in the dark." The same phrase appears in *The Mandragola* (V.2).

[84] *macatelle*: a meal of ground meatballs; later the word acquired the metaphorical meaning of "deceit," "fraud" or "defect." The phrase "play the *macatelle*" means to deceive by means of cleverness (Blasucci). Stage translation: ". . . how to play clever games!"

[85] or "have faith": *si fida*.

[86] I haven't . . . there: *io non vi ho tenute le mani*. Stage translation: "I haven't felt around to try and find out."

Apollonia,[87] I pray to you and all the patron saints and saintesses of matrimony to grant Clizia so much grace that from this bag will come the ballot of the one who will please us more!—Draw, in the name of God . . . Give it here . . . Oh no, I'm dead! It's "Eustachio"!

SOFRONIA: What is it? [*Aside*] Oh God, perform this miracle, so that he'll lose all hope.

NICOMACO: Draw from the other one. Give it here. The blank one! Ha! I'm brought back to life, we're victorious! Pirro, may it bring you good advantage; Eustachio has fallen dead. Sofronia, since God has willed that Clizia should belong to Pirro, you should will it too.

SOFRONIA: I will it.

NICOMACO: Arrange[88] the wedding.

SOFRONIA: You're in such a hurry. Couldn't it be delayed until tomorrow?

NICOMACO: No, no, no! Didn't you hear that? No! Why? Do you want to think up some trap?

SOFRONIA: Do we want to act like beasts? Doesn't she have to hear the conjugal mass?

NICOMACO: The bean mass! She can hear this another day! Don't you know that pardons are given to those who confess afterwards just as to those who confess beforehand?

SOFRONIA: Well, I'm worried that she may have what's ordinary for women.[89]

---

[87] Saint Apollonia—a holy virgin who suffered martyrdom in Alexandria during a local uprising against Christians in the third century—belongs to that class of Christian martyrs who voluntarily embraced the death prepared by their persecutors rather than renounce or compromise their faith. As a result of the beating and torture she endured before her death, Apollonia had all of her teeth knocked out, and so is invoked against toothaches and diseases of the teeth. This may make her an especially appropriate object of Nicomaco's prayer (cf. III.4; IV.2).

[88] arrange: *ordina.*

[89] what's ordinary for women: *l'ordinario delle donne*: menstruation.

NICOMACO: Well let her use the extraordinary of men![90] I intend for her to be married this evening. It seems that you don't understand me.

SOFRONIA: Marry her off then, into ruin. Let's go into the house, and *you* bring the poor girl this announcement, which won't be worth stockings.[91]

NICOMACO: It'll be worth pants.[92] Let's go inside.

SOFRONIA: [*Aside*] I don't want to go just yet, because I want to find Cleandro to see if he thinks there's some remedy for this evil.

Song

Whoever offends a woman,
whether wrongly or rightly, is a fool if he believes
that he will find in her, through prayers or complaints,[93] any
 kindness.
When she descends into this mortal life,
along with her soul she brings
great pride, anger and disregard of pardon;
trickery and cruelty are her escort,
and render her such aid
that in every enterprise she gratifies her desire;
and if anger harsh and wicked
moves her, or jealousy, she acts and looks on;
and her force surpasses all mortal force.

---

[90] the extraordinary of men: *lo straordinario degli uomini*: an obscene reference.

[91] worth stockings: referring to an ancient custom of giving stockings to the bearer of good news (Blasucci). Stage translation: ". . . won't be worth a tip."

[92] Stage translation: "It'll be worth a whole week's wages."

[93] prayers or complaints: *prieghi e pianti*.

ACT FOUR

Scene One
Cleandro, Eustachio

CLEANDRO: How is it possible that my mother could have been so thoughtless, submitting to chance[94] in this way a matter on which the honor of our household completely depends?

EUSTACHIO: It's as I told you.

CLEANDRO: Oh, my misfortune! Oh, my unhappiness! You see, I ran into just the person to detain me long enough so that without my knowing it this marriage was concluded and the wedding decided on. Everything has gone according to the old man's desire! Oh fortune, since you're a woman, you're customarily the friend of young men, but this time you've been a friend of the old![95] Aren't you ashamed to have arranged for such a delicate face to be slobbered on by such a smelly mouth, such delicate flesh to be touched by such trembling hands, such wrinkled and stinking limbs? Because it isn't Pirro, but rather Nicomaco, as I judge it, who'll possess her. You couldn't have done me a greater injury! With this blow you've taken from me my love and my property, for, if this love lasts, Nicomaco will surely leave more of his wealth to Pirro than to me. Oh, it seems to be taking a thousand years for me to spot my mother. I need to complain to her and get this situation off my chest.

EUSTACHIO: Take some comfort, Cleandro, from the fact that she seemed to me to be snickering as she went into the

---

[94] chance: *sorta*: lot or luck.

[95] Cf. *The Prince*, xxv: "fortune is a woman . . . and, as a woman, she is a friend of the young, because they are less respectful, more ferocious, and command her with greater boldness" (my translation).

house, and so it seems certain to me that the old man isn't going to pick this pear as cleanly as he believes. But here he comes with Pirro, and they're both cheerful.

CLEANDRO: Go into the house, Eustachio. I want to stay here, off to the side, to hear some of their council that may prove to be of use to me.

EUSTACHIO: I'm going.

Scene Two
Nicomaco, Pirro, Cleandro

NICOMACO: [*To Pirro*] Oh, how well it has gone! Did you see how sad the whole crowd was, and how my wife despaired? All of this increases my good cheer. But I'll be much more cheerful when I hold Clizia in my arms, when I touch her, kiss her and squeeze her. Oh sweet night, will I ever make it to you? And this debt that I have to you, I'm going to pay it to you double!

CLEANDRO: [*Hiding. Aside*] Oh, the crazy old man!

PIRRO: I believe it, but I don't really believe that you'll be able to do anything this evening, nor do I see any opportunity there.

NICOMACO: Why not? I'll tell you how I plan to manage[96] the matter.

PIRRO: I'd appreciate that.

CLEANDRO: [*Aside*] So would I, much more, because I might hear something that would spoil the affairs of others and repair my own.

NICOMACO: You know Damone, my neighbor, whose house I've rented on your account?

PIRRO: Yes, I know him.

---

[96] manage: *governare*: lit. "govern."

NICOMACO: I've come up with the plan that you'll take her to that house this evening, even though he's still living there and hasn't moved out yet, for I'll say that I want you to take her to the house where she's going to live.

PIRRO: What'll happen next?

CLEANDRO: [Aside] Prick up your ears, Cleandro!

NICOMACO: I've directed my wife to call on Sostrata, Damone's wife, to help her arrange this wedding and prepare the new bride, and I'll tell Damone to urge his wife to go. After this has been done, and when supper is over, the bride will be taken by this woman to Damone's house and placed with you in the room, in bed. And I'll say that I'm going to stay with Damone at a hotel, and Sostrata will come stay with Sofronia here in our house. When you're alone in the room, you'll put out the light and fumble around the room, making it look like you're getting undressed; meanwhile, I'll come into the room very quietly, get undressed and get into bed with Clizia. You can remain quietly on the couch. In the morning, before dawn, pretending that I need to pee, I'll get out of bed and get dressed again, and you can get into bed.

CLEANDRO: [Aside] Oh, you old rascal! How fortunate it is for me[97] to hear this plan of yours! And how unlucky for you[98] that I've heard it!

PIRRO: It seems to me that you've handled this business well. But you'd better arm yourself so that you'll appear young, because I'm worried that your old age will be noticed even in the dark.

CLEANDRO: [Aside] I've heard enough. I need to go and report this to my mother.

[Exit]

---

[97] how fortunate it is for me: *quanta è stata la mia felicità.*

[98] how unlucky for you: *quanta la tua disgrazia.*

NICOMACO: I've thought of everything, and I intend, to tell you the truth, to have supper with Damone, and I've arranged for a supper of my own devising. First, I'll take a dose of a potion called satyrion.[99]

PIRRO: What kind of strange name is that?

NICOMACO: It has stranger effects! Because it's a potion that, so far as this business is concerned, would rejuvenate a man of ninety, let alone one of seventy like myself. After taking this potion, I'll eat a few things, but all of them substantial. First, a salad of cooked onions; next, a mixture of beans and spices.

PIRRO: What does this do?

NICOMACO: What does it do? These onions, beans and spices, because they're hot and windy, would make a Genoan frigate set sail. On top of this, I'll have a fat roasted pigeon, so undercooked that it'll bleed a bit.

PIRRO: Watch out that you don't spoil your stomach, because you'll need to have someone chew this for you, or else you'll have to swallow it whole: I don't see very many, or very strong, teeth in that mouth of yours!

NICOMACO: I'm not worried about this, for while I don't have many teeth, I've got jaws like steel.

PIRRO: I think that after you've gone and I get into bed, I'll be able to get by without touching her, since I have a vision of finding that poor girl broken into pieces.

NICOMACO: It's enough for you that I'll have done your duty, and that of a companion as well.

PIRRO: I thank God, because he's given me a wife in such a way that I won't have to work hard either to get her pregnant or to pay her expenses.

---

[99]satyrion: a drink made from a type of orchid whose sap acts as an aphrodisiac (Blasucci).

NICOMACO: Go into the house, urge on the wedding, and I'll go speak a bit with Damone, whom I see coming out of his house.

PIRRO: I'll do this.

Scene Three
Nicomaco, Damone

NICOMACO: The time has come, Damone, for you to show if you're my friend. You have to move out of your house, and don't leave either your wife or any other person there, because I want to manage[100] this matter as I've already told you.

DAMONE: I'm prepared to do everything, however I may satisfy you.

NICOMACO: I've told my wife to call on your Sostrata to come and help her arrange the wedding. Make sure she comes straightaway when she's called, and above all that she comes with her maid.

DAMONE: Everything's arranged.[101] Call her whenever you're ready.

NICOMACO: I have to go over to the druggist to do some business, and I'll return right away. You wait here for my wife to come out and call yours. Here she comes; be prepared. So long.

Scene Four
Sofronia, Damone

SOFRONIA: [*Aside*] I'm not amazed that my husband urged me to call on Sostrata, Damone's wife! He wants to free up the house so that he can joust there as he pleases. Here's

---

[100] manage: *governare*: lit. "govern."

[101]arranged: *ordinato*.

Damone. Oh, this model of the city, pillar of his community, who lets out his house for such an indecent and disgraceful enterprise! But I'll handle them in such a way that they'll always be ashamed of themselves. But now I want to start having some fun with him.[102]

DAMONE: [*Aside*] I'm amazed that Sofronia's standing still and isn't coming forward to call on my wife. Oh, here she comes.

[*To Sofronia*]

God save you, Sofronia!

SOFRONIA: And you, Damone! Where's your wife?

DAMONE: She's in the house, and she's ready to come if you call on her, because your husband asked me about this. Should I go call her?

SOFRONIA: No, no! She must have business to attend to.

DAMONE: She doesn't have any business.

SOFRONIA: Leave her alone, I don't want to give her any trouble. I'll call her when it's time.

DAMONE: Aren't you arranging the wedding?

SOFRONIA: Yes, we're arranging it.

DAMONE: Isn't there some necessity for someone to help you?

SOFRONIA: There's a whole world of a crowd in there right now.

DAMONE: [*Aside*] What'll I do now? I've made a huge mistake on account of that crazy, drooling, bleary-eyed, toothless old man. He's made me offer my wife to help her, yet she doesn't want her, so that now she'll believe that I'm begging for a meal and she'll think me a wretch.

[*Exit*]

SOFRONIA: I'm leaving him here all wrapped up in confusion. Look how he goes away, pulling his cloak around him! Now

---

[102]having some fun with: *uccellare*. The word literally refers to fowling or hunting birds with snares, and so it can also mean "deceive," "hoodwink" or "lay a trap."

it remains for me to have a bit of fun with that old man of mine. Here he is, coming from the market. I'll die if he hasn't bought something to make him appear vigorous, sweet-smelling!

Scene Five
Nicomaco, Sofronia

NICOMACO: [*Aside*] I've bought the potion and a certain ointment fit to wake up the brigades. When one goes into war armed, one goes with more spiritedness by half. I see my wife. Oh dear, she must have heard[103] me!

SOFRONIA: [*Aside*] Yes, I heard you, and it'll be to your loss and shame, if I live until tomorrow!

NICOMACO: Have things been arranged? Did you call on this neighbor of yours to help you?

SOFRONIA: I called on her, as you told me. But this dear friend of yours said I don't know what in her ear, so that she answered me that she couldn't come.

NICOMACO: I'm not amazed by this, because you're a little rude and you don't know how to be agreeable with people when you want something from them.

SOFRONIA: What did you want me to do, stroke him under the chin? I'm not used to caressing other people's husbands. You go call on her, since you're good at going after other people's wives, and I'll go into the house to arrange the rest.

Scene Six
Damone, Nicomaco

DAMONE: [*Aside*] I'm coming to see if this lover has returned from the market. But here he is, in front of his door.

---

[103]heard: *sentito*: also "perceived" or "smelled."

[*To Nicomaco*]

I've just been coming to see you.

NICOMACO: And I you, you good-for-nothing man! What did I beg you to do? What did I ask of you? You've served me so well!

DAMONE: What's the matter?

NICOMACO: You sent your wife! You emptied the crowd from your house, and were delighted to do it! You did all of this so well that on account of you I'm dead and undone!

DAMONE: Go hang yourself! Didn't you tell me that your wife would call on mine?

NICOMACO: She did call on her, and you wouldn't let her come.

DAMONE: Not at all! The offer was made to her! But she didn't want her to come, and so she made fun of me and now you complain to me. The devil take you, and this wedding, and everyone!

NICOMACO: In short, do you want her to come?

DAMONE: Yes, I want her to go, and be damned! Her and her maid and the cat and whoever else is there! Go, if you have anything else to do. I'll go into the house and send her right away through the backyard.

[*Exit*]

NICOMACO: Now he's my friend, now things will go well! Oh dear, oh dear, what's that noise I hear in the house?

Scene Seven
Doria, Nicomaco

DORIA: [*Coming out of the house, shouting*] I'm dying, I'm dying! Run, run! Take that knife out of her hand! Run, Sofronia!

NICOMACO: What's the matter with you, Doria? What is it?

DORIA: I'm dying!

NICOMACO: Why are you dying?

DORIA: I'm dying, and you're all finished!

NICOMACO: Tell me what's wrong with you.

DORIA: I can't, I'm so out of breath! I'm sweating! Fan a bit of wind on me with your cloak!

NICOMACO: Come on! Tell me what's wrong, before I bash your head in!

DORIA: Oh my master, you're too cruel!

NICOMACO: Tell me what's the matter, and what that noise is in the house.

DORIA: Well, Pirro had just given the ring to Clizia and gone to accompany the notary to the back door. Well, don't you know that Clizia, moved by I don't know what passion,[104] picked up a dagger, and completely wild,[105] all in a fury, shouted: "Where's Nicomaco? Where's Pirro? I'm going to kill them!" Cleandro, Sofronia, all of us, wanted to catch her, but we couldn't. She's backed herself into a corner of the room and she's shouting that she wants to kill you no matter what, and out of fear one runs here, another there. Pirro has fled into the kitchen and hidden himself behind the capon basket. I was sent here to warn you not to come into the house.

NICOMACO: I'm the most miserable of all men! Can't the dagger be taken from her hand?

DORIA: No, not yet.

NICOMACO: Whom is she threatening?

DORIA: You and Pirro.

NICOMACO: Oh, what misfortune this is! Come now, dear child, I beg you, go back into the house and with good words see if you can lift this craziness from her head and get her to put down the dagger, and I promise you that I'll buy you a pair of shoes and a kerchief. Come now, go, my love!

---

[104]passion: *furia*.

[105]wild: *scapigliata*: disheveled, intemperate, dissolute.

DORIA: I'm going. But don't come into the house unless I call you.

[*Goes into house*]

NICOMACO: Oh, my misery, oh, my misfortune! How many things have thwarted me and make unhappy this night which I expected to be most happy!

[*Calling inside*]

Has she put down the knife? Should I come in?

DORIA: [*Shouting, from inside*] Not yet, don't come in!

NICOMACO: Oh God, what'll happen next?

[*Calling inside*]

Can I come in?

DORIA: [*Appearing at the door*] Come in, but don't go into the room where she is. Make sure she doesn't see you: go into the kitchen next to Pirro.

NICOMACO: I'm going.

Scene Eight
Doria alone

In how many ways we've made fun of this old man! What a festival it is to see the troubles of this household! The old man and Pirro are terrified in the kitchen, in the hall are those who are preparing the supper, and in the room are the women, Cleandro and the rest of the family. They've undressed Siro, our servant, and in his clothes they've dressed Clizia and in Clizia's clothes they've dressed Siro, and they plan to have Siro go to the groom in place of Clizia. And so that the old man and Pirro won't discover this fraud, they've confined them in the kitchen with the story[106] that Clizia is full of wrath. What a fine laugh! What a beautiful trick! But here are Nicomaco and Pirro outside.

---

[106]with the story: *sotto ombra*: lit. "under the shadow."

Scene Nine
Nicomaco, Doria, Pirro

NICOMACO: What are you doing over there, Doria? Has Clizia been quieted?

DORIA: Yes Sir, and she's promised Sofronia that she intends to do as you wish. And it's very true that Sofronia judges that it would be good for you and Pirro not to confront her, so that her anger won't flare up again. Later, after she's been put to bed, if Pirro doesn't know how to tame her, that'll be his problem.

NICOMACO: Sofronia has counseled us well, and we'll do it this way. Now go into the house, and since everything has been cooked, urge them to have supper. Pirro and I will have supper at Damone's house. When they've finished supper, have her brought outside. Urge it on, Doria, for the love of God, because nine o'clock[107] has already sounded, and it's not good to keep these dealings going on all night.

DORIA: What you say is true. I'm going.

[*Exit*]

NICOMACO: You, Pirro, stay here while I go and have a drop to drink with Damone. Don't go into the house, so that Clizia won't be infuriated anew. And if anything happens, run to tell me.

PIRRO: Go on, and I'll do as you direct me.

[*Nicomaco exits*]
[*In soliloquy*]

Since my master wants me to be without a wife and without supper, I'm content. I don't believe that in a whole year as many things could happen as have already happened here today; but I'm worried that still other things may happen to me, because I've heard some loud laughter coming from the house and I'm not pleased by it. But here I see a torch

---

[107]nine o'clock: the text reads "three o'clock." See note 54 above.

appearing: the procession must be coming out, the bride must be coming. I have to run to get the old man.

[*Shouting up to Damone's house*]

Nicomaco, hey, Damone, come down, down! The bride's coming!

Scene Ten
Nicomaco, Damone, Sofronia, Sostrata

NICOMACO: Here we are. Pirro, go into the house; I believe it's good that she not see you. Damone, put yourself in front of me and speak with these women. Here they all are outside.

SOFRONIA: Oh, poor girl, she keeps crying! See how she doesn't lift her kerchief from her eyes.

Sostrata: She'll laugh tomorrow! That's how it's customary for girls to behave. God give you good evening, Nicomaco and Damone!

DAMONE: And welcome to you. Go upstairs, ladies, put the girl to bed, and then come back down. Meanwhile Pirro will be getting himself in order too.

Sostrata: Let's go, in the name of God.

Scene Eleven
Nicomaco, Damone

NICOMACO: She goes with such sadness. But did you see how tall she was? She must be aided by high-heeled shoes.

DAMONE: She also looked bigger than usual. Oh Nicomaco, you're so fortunate! The affair has been brought to where you want it. But handle yourself well, or else you won't be able to go back for more!

NICOMACO: Don't worry, I'm ready to do what needs doing! Since I had that food, I feel as strong as a sword. But here are the women returning.

Scene Twelve
Nicomaco, Sostrata, Sofronia, Damone

NICOMACO: Have you put her to bed?

SOSTRATA: Yes, we have.

DAMONE: Good. We'll do the rest. Sostrata, you go sleep with Sofronia, and Nicomaco will stay here with me.

SOFRONIA: Let's go, for they act as if it's taking them a thousand years to get rid of us.

DAMONE: And the same to you. Watch out that you don't hurt each other.

SOSTRATA: You're the ones who'd better watch out, since you've got the weapons. We're unarmed.

DAMONE: Let's go into the house.

SOFRONIA: We'll go too. [*Aside*] Go Nicomaco, to where you'll come upon an obstacle. For this woman of yours will be like the pitchers of Santa Maria Impruneta.[108]

Song[109]

So pleasing is the trick
conducted to its dear, imagined end,
that strips others of their worries
and makes every bitter taste sweet.
Oh, remedy high and rare,
you show the straight path to wandering souls;
you, with your great worth,
in making others blessed you make Love rich;
you conquer, by means of your holy counsels alone,
stones, venoms and spells.

---

[108]The pitchers made at Impruneta, near Florence, had a characteristic spout or spigot that stuck out erect from the underside (Guerri).

[109]The same song appears at the end of act III of *The Mandragola*.

ACT FIVE

Scene One
Doria alone

I've never laughed so much, and I don't believe that I'll laugh so much ever again; nor, in our household on this night, has anyone done anything except laugh. Sofronia, Sostrata, Cleandro, Eustachio, everyone laughed. The night was spent in measuring the time, and they said: "Now Nicomaco's going into the room, now he's getting undressed, now he's lying down beside the bride, now he's starting to battle her, now he's locked in vigorous combat." And while we were occupied with these thoughts, Siro and Pirro arrived at the house, and they redoubled our laughter. And the finest thing to see was Pirro laughing at Siro, so much so that I don't believe that anyone has had a finer or better pleasure this year. Those women have sent me outside, since it's already dawn, to see what the old man's doing, and how he's bearing this disaster. But here he is outside with Damone. I'm going to stand off to the side, to see if I can get some matter to laugh about anew.

Scene Two
Damone, Nicomaco, Doria

DAMONE: What's been happening all night? How did it go? You're silent. What was all that commotion, of getting dressed, opening the door, getting down from and jumping up into bed? You never kept still! And since I was in bed in a room on the ground floor beneath you I couldn't sleep at all, so, disgusted, I got up, and now I find that you've come outside all upset. You're not speaking; you look dead to me. What the devil is wrong with you?

NICOMACO: My brother, I don't know where I can run, where I can hide, or where I can conceal this great shame I've incurred. I'm disgraced for eternity, I have no further remedy, and I can't ever again face my wife, my children, my relatives, my servants. I went in search of my disgrace and

53

my wife helped me find it, and now it's all over for me. And it pains me so much more because you'll also have a share of my bad name,[110] for everyone will know that you had a hand in this.

DAMONE: What happened? Did you break something?

NICOMACO: What would you like me to have broken? I wish that I'd broken my neck!

DAMONE: What happened, then? Why won't you tell me?

NICOMACO: [*Crying*] Uhh, uhh, uhh! I have so much grief that I don't believe I can tell you about it.

DAMONE: Come on, you look like a baby! Good Lord, what could it be?

NICOMACO: You know the arrangement[111] that was laid down. Following this arrangement, I went into the room and quietly got undressed, and, when the light had been put out, in place of Pirro who took his place on the couch to sleep, I lay down beside the bride.

DAMONE: Well now, what happened then?

NICOMACO: Uhh, uhh, uhh! I got close to her, and following the custom of new husbands I went to put my hands on her breasts, but she took hold of me with her hand and wouldn't let me. I went to kiss her, and with her other hand she pushed my face away. I went to throw myself all over her, and she gave me a shot with her knee, so hard that she broke one of my ribs. When I saw that force wouldn't be enough, I turned to pleading, and with sweet, loving words—in a quiet voice, so that she wouldn't recognize me—I begged her to be so kind as to please me, saying to her: "Come, my sweet soul, why do you torture me? Come, my dear, why don't you concede to me willingly what other wives concede willingly to their husbands?" Uhh, uhh, uhh!

---

[110] bad name: *carico.*

[111] arrangement: *ordine.*

DAMONE: Dry your eyes a bit.

NICOMACO: I have so much grief that there's no place to put it, and I can't hold back my tears. I just went on chattering, but she never gave any sign of wanting to speak to me, let alone anything else. Now, seeing this, I turned to threats and I began to speak foul abuses, about what I would both do to her and say to her. Well, don't you know that all at once she gathered up her legs and threw me a couple of kicks, and if the bed cover hadn't held me, I would've been hurled into the middle of the floor!

DAMONE: Can it be?

NICOMACO: Indeed it can! After she had done this, she turned on her face and held herself tight with her breast on the mattress, so that all the winches in the Opera couldn't have turned her over.[112] And, seeing that force, pleas and threats were of no use to me, out of desperation I turned my back on her and decided to leave her alone, thinking that towards dawn she might change her mind.

DAMONE: Oh, you did well! You ought to have taken this route in the first place: if she didn't want you, don't want her!

NICOMACO: Hold on, it didn't end there. Now comes the best part! In my bewilderment I began—owing to the grief and strain I'd had—to fall asleep a bit. Well, don't you know that all at once I felt myself being stabbed in the flank and being given five or six accursed shots under the rump! And, half asleep as I was, I immediately put my hand down there and found something firm and pointy, and so, completely terrified, I jumped out of bed, remembering the dagger that Clizia had taken to give to me. At this noise Pirro, who was sleeping, got up, and I told him—being driven more by fear

---

[112] all the winches in the Opera: a reference to the Opera del Duomo. The Duomo is the most recognizable cathedral in Florence, famous for its domed cupola designed by the Renaissance architect Filippo Brunelleschi. The Opera del Duomo was an administrative body created in 1296 to oversee the construction and maintenance of the cathedral.

than by reason—to run and get a light because she was armed to kill us both. Pirro ran, and when he returned with a light we saw, instead of Clizia, Siro, my servant, upright on the bed, entirely naked, and he in contempt—uhh, uhh, uhh!—made faces at me and then—uhh, uhh, uhh!—the *manichetto*![113]

DAMONE: Ha, ha, ha!

NICOMACO: What Damone, are you laughing?

DAMONE: I'm very sorry about this case, but it's impossible not to laugh.

DORIA: [*Aside*] I'm going to report what I've heard to the mistress,[114] so that her laughter may be redoubled.

[*Exit*]

NICOMACO: This is my misfortune, that can bring laughter to everyone and tears to me. Even Pirro and Siro, in my presence, would first utter foul abuses to each other, and then would laugh. Then, dressed as they were with their backsides bare, they went away, and I believe they've gone to find the women and that all of them must be laughing. And so everyone laughs, and Nicomaco cries!

DAMONE: I believe that you believe that I'm very sorry for you, and for myself as well, since, out of love for you, I got myself into this maze.

NICOMACO: What do you advise me to do? Don't abandon me, for the love of God!

DAMONE: It seems to me, if something better doesn't come up, that you should put yourself completely in the hands of your Sofronia and tell her that from now on she may do as she wishes with both Clizia and you. She also ought to think about your honor, because, since you're her husband, you can't have any shame that she won't share in too. Here she

---

[113] *manichetto*: an obscene gesture formed by placing the left hand inside the elbow of the bent right arm while thrusting the right fist into the air. Stage translation: "and then he gave me the finger!"

[114] mistress: *la padrona*: fem. of *padrone*, "master."

comes outside. Go, speak to her. Meanwhile, I'll go to the public square and to the market to see if I can hear anything about this case, and I'll start covering up for you as much as I can.

NICOMACO: I beg you to do this.

Scene Three
Sofronia, Nicomaco

SOFRONIA: [*Carrying a basket of food*] Doria, my maid, told me that Nicomaco's outside and that he's a pitiful sight[115] to see. I'm going to speak with him, to see what he'll say to me about this new case. There he is. Oh, Nicomaco!

NICOMACO: What do you want?

SOFRONIA: Where are you going at such an early hour? Did you leave the house without saying a word to the bride? Do you know how it went last night with Pirro?

NICOMACO: I don't know.

SOFRONIA: Who does know, if you don't, you who made Florence go bottoms up in order to bring about this marriage? Now that it's done, you pretend not to know anything[116] about it and to be discontent!

NICOMACO: Come on, leave me alone! Don't torment me!

SOFRONIA: You're the one who's tormenting me, because, while you ought to be comforting me, I have to comfort you, and while you ought to be providing for them, it falls to me to do so, for you see that I'm bringing them these eggs.

NICOMACO: I believe it's good for you not to want to make a complete joke out of me. It's enough for you to have had it so all this past year, and yesterday, and last night more than ever.

---

[115] pitiful sight: *una compassione.*

[116] pretend not to know anything: *tu te mostri nuovo.*

SOFRONIA: I never wanted you to be a joke, but you're the one who wanted it for all the rest of us, and in the end for yourself! Aren't you ashamed to have raised a young girl in your house with so much decency and in the manner that daughters of respectable people are raised, and then to want to marry her off to a wicked and useless servant just because he was content to have you lie with her? Did you really believe that you were dealing with the blind and with people who didn't know how to put a stop to the indecency of your designs? I confess that I've orchestrated all these tricks that have been played on you, because if I wanted to make you repent there was no other way than to have you enter into a deed with so many witnesses that you'd be ashamed of it, and then the shame would make you do what nothing else could have made you do. Now the affair has come to this: If you're willing to return to the mark, and to be the Nicomaco that you were one year ago, all of us will go back there and the matter won't be made known; and even if it is known about, it's customary to err and to be corrected.

NICOMACO: My dear Sofronia, do as you wish. I'm prepared not to go outside your arrangements,[117] provided that the matter isn't made known.

SOFRONIA: If you're willing to do this, everything's settled.

NICOMACO: Clizia, where is she?

SOFRONIA: I sent her away—as soon as supper was over yesterday evening, dressed in Siro's clothes—to a convent.

NICOMACO: Cleandro, what does he say?

SOFRONIA: He's cheerful because this wedding was spoiled, but he's very pained because he doesn't see how he can get Clizia.

---

[117] arrangements: *ordini.*

NICOMACO: I'll leave it to you now to plan Cleandro's affairs. Nevertheless, unless we know where she comes from, it doesn't seem to me that we can give her to him.

SOFRONIA: It doesn't seem so to me either. We must put off marrying her until something is known about her, or until he comes out of this fantasy[118] of his. Meanwhile, the marriage to Pirro will be annulled.

NICOMACO: Manage it[119] as you wish. I'm going into the house to get some rest, because with the bad night I've had I can't stand up straight, and also because I see Cleandro and Eustachio coming outside and I don't want to talk with them. You speak with them. Tell them the conclusion we've reached, that it's enough for them to have won, and that they're not to discuss this case with me any more.

Scene Four
Cleandro, Sofronia, Eustachio

CLEANDRO: [*To Eustachio*] You heard how the old man went and shut himself up in the house. He must have had a good scolding from Sofronia, he looks so humble! Let's go to her to hear about the matter.

[*To Sofronia*]
God save you, my dear mother! What did Nicomaco say?

SOFRONIA: He's completely humiliated, the poor man; he thinks himself disgraced. He's given me a free hand,[120] and he wants me to manage[121] everything in the future according to my judgment.

EUSTACHIO: This'll be fine! I'm going to get Clizia!

CLEANDRO: Slow up a bit! She's not a morsel for you.

---

[118] *fantasia*. See note 30 above.

[119] manage it: *governala*: lit. "govern it."

[120] a free hand: *el foglio bianco*: lit. "a white page" (cognate: "carte blanche").

[121] manage: *governi*: lit. "govern."

EUSTACHIO: Oh, this is just beautiful! Now, when I believe I've won, am I going to lose, just like Pirro?

SOFRONIA: Neither you nor Pirro will have her. Nor will you, Cleandro, because I want it this way.

CLEANDRO: At least have her come back home, so that I won't be deprived of seeing her.

SOFRONIA: She'll come back, or she won't come back, however will seem best to me. Let's go get the house back in shape. And you, Cleandro, see if you can find Damone, because it'll be good to speak with him, for it remains to see how this case that's occurred has to be covered up.

CLEANDRO: I'm discontent.

SOFRONIA: You can be content some other time!

Scene Five
Cleandro alone

Just when I believed that I'd arrived safely in port,[122] fortune throws me back into the middle of the sea, into still rougher and stormier waves! First I battled against my father's love, and now I'm battling against my mother's ambition. Against the former I had her as help, but against this latter I'm alone, and so I see less light in this than I saw in that. I lament my bad luck, since I was born never to have anything good. And I can say that since this girl came to our house I've known no other delights than those that come from thinking about her, for there the pleasures have been so rare that their days could easily be counted. But who's this I see coming towards me? Is it Damone? Yes, it's him, and he's all cheerful. What is it, Damone? What news are you bringing? Where's all this cheerfulness coming from?

---

[122] arrived safely in port: *essere navigato.*

Scene Six
Damone, Cleandro

DAMONE: No better news, nor any happier, nor any that I would bring more willingly, could I have heard!

CLEANDRO: What is it?

DAMONE: The father of your Clizia has arrived in this city. He's named R̲a̲m̲o̲n̲d̲o̲, he's a Neapolitan gentleman, he's wealthy, and he's come solely to find his daughter again.

CLEANDRO: How do you know this?

DAMONE: I know it because I've spoken with him and heard everything. There's no doubt at all.

CLEANDRO: How can it be? I'm crazy with good cheer.

DAMONE: I want you all to hear it from him. Call Nicomaco outside, and Sofronia your mother.

CLEANDRO: [*Calling upstairs*] Sofronia, oh Nicomaco! Come downstairs to see Damone.

Scene Seven
Nicomaco, Damone, Sofronia, Ramondo

NICOMACO: Here we are! What's the good news?

DAMONE: I say that Clizia's father, named Ramondo, a Neapolitan gentleman, is in Florence to find her again. I've spoken with him, and I've already persuaded him to give her as a wife to Cleandro, if you're willing.

NICOMACO: If this is so, I'm very content with it. But where is he?

DAMONE: At the Crown; I told him to come here. Here he comes. He's the one with all those servants behind him! Let's go meet him.

NICOMACO: Here we are.

[*To Ramondo*]
God save you, good man![123]

---

[123] good man. See note 21 above.

DAMONE: Ramondo, this is Nicomaco and his wife, who have raised your daughter with so much honor. And this is their son, who'll be your son-in-law, if it pleases you.

RAMONDO: I'm so glad to meet you all! And I thank God that he's given me so much grace that, before I die, I may see my daughter again and reward these gentlemen who have honored her. As for the marriage, nothing could gratify me more, for in this way the friendship that has been started between us owing to your merits may be maintained by means of the marriage.

DAMONE: Let's go inside, where you can hear from Ramondo the whole story in detail and make arrangements for this happy wedding.

SOFRONIA: Let's go!

[*To audience*]

And you spectators, you can go home, because, without coming outside any more, we'll arrange the new wedding, which will be feminine, not masculine like that of Nicomaco!

Song

You beautiful souls, who so attentively and quietly
have listened to this decent, humble example,
this wise and noble teacher
of our human life,
and through it have come to know
what one ought to shun, what pursue,
in order to ascend straight up to heaven,
and who, under a thin veil
a good deal more have heard (that now would take too
  long to tell);
Come, we pray that you will have that profit
which your great courtesy deserves.

SECRET
FREQUENCIES:
A NEW YORK EDUCATION

John Skoyles

University of Nebraska Press
Lincoln and London

Acknowledgments for the use of
previously published material ap-
pear on page vii. | © 2003 by
the Board of Regents of the Uni-
versity of Nebraska | All rights
reserved | Manufactured in the
United States of America

Library of Congress Cataloging-in-
Publication Data

Skoyles, John.
Secret frequencies : a New York
education / John Skoyles.
p.   cm. — (American lives)
ISBN 0-8032-4304-9 (cloth : alk.
paper)
1. Skoyles, John—Childhood
and youth.   2. New York (N.Y.)—
Biography.   3. Teenage boys—
New York (State)—New York—
Biography.   4. New York
(N.Y.)—Social life and customs—
20th century.   5. City and town
life—New York (State)—New
York.   I. Title.   II. Series.
F128.57.S56 S43 2003
974.7'1043' '092—dc21
                    2003000600